William Anderson

Filial Honour of God

by confidence, obedience and resignation - with appendices on the reward of grace

and on the nature of the cup of Gethsemane

William Anderson

Filial Honour of God
by confidence, obedience and resignation - with appendices on the reward of grace and on the nature of the cup of Gethsemane

ISBN/EAN: 9783337193492

Printed in Europe, USA, Canada, Australia, Japan

Cover: Foto ©Lupo / pixelio.de

More available books at **www.hansebooks.com**

FILIAL HONOUR OF GOD

BY

CONFIDENCE, OBEDIENCE, AND RESIGNATION.

WITH APPENDICES ON THE REWARD OF GRACE, AND ON THE NATURE OF THE CUP OF GETHSEMANE.

By WILLIAM ANDERSON, LL.D.,
GLASGOW.

LONDON:
HODDER & STOUGHTON, 27 PATERNOSTER ROW.
MDCCCLXX.

CONTENTS.

	PAGE.
PREFATORY NOTICE,	vii
INTRODUCTORY,	1
CONFIDENCE,	8-12
OBEDIENCE,	12-91
RESIGNATION,	91-162

APPENDIX A.—TESTIMONIES TO THE DOCTRINE OF THE REWARD OF GOOD WORKS.

SECTION FIRST:—TESTIMONIES OF CONFESSIONS OF THE CHURCHES OF THE REFORMATION.

AUGSBURG AND HELVETIC CONFESSIONS, &c.,	163
CALVIN'S CATECHISM,	166

SECTION SECOND:—INDIVIDUAL TESTIMONIES OF THE OLDER THEOLOGIANS.

CALVIN'S INSTITUTES,	168
TURRETIN'S INSTITUTION,	174
MACCOVIUS'S COMMON PLACES,	177
WITSIUS'S ECONOMY,	178

SECTION THIRD:—TESTIMONIES OF MODERN THEOLOGIANS.

DWIGHT'S THEOLOGY,	180
DICK'S THEOLOGY,	180
HILL'S LECTURES ON DIVINITY,	181
CHALMERS'S INSTITUTES OF THEOLOGY,	182
CUNNINGHAM'S HISTORICAL THEOLOGY,	186
WARDLAW'S SYSTEMATIC THEOLOGY,	186
RUSSELL'S LETTERS,	189

CONTENTS.

TESTIMONIES OF THE SECEDERS OF SCOTLAND.

Introductory,	191
Ebenezer and Ralph Erskines,	193
Dr. George Lawson,	204
Dr. John Brown,	208
Dr. William Lindsay,	208
Dr. N. M'Michael,	209
Dr. John Eadie,	210
Rev. J. Hay,	210
Rev. Alexander Jack,	211
Dr. Andrew Sommerville,	211
Dr. John Mitchell,	213

TESTIMONIES OF ENGLISH NON-CONFORMISTS.

Rev. Robert Hall,	214
Dr. Richard Winter Hamilton,	216
Rev. Thomas Binney,	218
Rev. Richard Watson,	220

EPISCOPALIAN TESTIMONY.

Dr. James O'Brien,	221

APPENDIX B.—GETHSEMANE.

What was the Cup from the Drinking of which Christ Prayed, if it were possible, He might be Saved? — 225-249

PREFATORY NOTICE.

THE peculiar nature of the following Descant, or by whatever name it may be characterised, needs an explanation. In the course of preparing a companion volume to two, formerly published, of promiscuous Discourses, The Filial Honouring of God was one of the selected subjects; but the illustrations increased to such an extent as to make them unsuitable for a volume of such variety as I designed; and I was about to lay them aside, when friends who had heard them preached advised that I should publish them in a volume by themselves, and leave the promiscuous volume in abeyance. I adopted this counsel, but resolved to remodel the illustrations by making *excursions* into controversial fields (especially those two, The Reward of a Saint's Good Works, and The Nature of the Cup of Gethsemane) which I could only *skirt* in popular discourse. The result has been that I fear those polemical excursions may so engage the attention as to withdraw it from the practical, experimental, and consolatory portions by which the illustrations were originally characterised.

As regards the first of these excursions—on the Reward of Good Works—though there had been a likelihood of my orthodoxy being questioned, it would have given me little concern; but there will not be any such attempt. Zealotry must dispose of the Confessors of Augsburg, Calvin, Turretin, the Westminster Divines, Ralph Wardlaw, David Russell, Robert Hall, George Lawson, R. Winter Hamilton, Thomas Binney, James O'Brien, and a great many others of theological might and renown, before it reach me with heretical imputations. It will not attempt this. But here is what it will do—I know well what spirit it is of—it will say, See what an unchristian temper of bitterness he betrays (itself being so sweetly charitable)! I reply by anticipation, See what Dr. Chalmers says of you! (*Vide* p. 182.) He denounces you as being a multitude of pestilent antinomians, whom he commissions his students to go forth and abolish with unrelenting vengeance; whereas I have laboured to defend you from what I regard as being an over-charged impeachment; for, honestly, I do not think you are so bad as he calls you.*

* Just as the press was about to give its finishing stroke to my Book, I have arrested it for the insertion of the following Testimony on the subject of the Reward of good works, given by Dr. Chalmers, when, retired from his academic office, in which he gave utterance to opinions which I have censured, he was now grappling with the question of his personal salvation, in a manner so trying of himself, and so trying of all, of any spirituality of mind, who read the record of his mental exercise and conflict.—The extract is the vindication at once of what I have said of his Institutes (*Vide* p. 184), and of what I have said of Zealots:—

"Let me not forego the motive to good works which lies in the comfort and encouragement of their being acceptable to Thee, through Jesus Christ. There is a certain orthodox antipathy to the very name of Reward, and a certain forbidding glance cast at it by those in authority and possessing the estimation of those who are Masters in Israel, which have practically the effect of an interdict, or, at least, a chilling influence on all

As regards the other of my principal polemical excursions—on the Nature of the Cup of Gethsemane, I now regret that I should have mentioned Markland, good though his authority be, as a coadjutor in this contention of vindicating the character of Christ from the imputation, that, in a state of natural tremor, He momentarily lost his faith, and prayed for *that* as being perhaps possible, which life-long He was convinced it was impossible to grant Him, unless He threw up the commission of being the World's Redeemer. I feel confident that I have delivered the Faith from this great enormity; and would rather that I had reserved the credit of having done so "single-handed," without the aid of any other name.

Though not necessary (for my argument is sufficient without it), yet for logical completeness I have explained how the human nature of our Lord could suffer mentally, though united with the divine. We accuse Socinians of having abolished his Divinity; they have reason for retorting that some of us abolish his Humanity. Essentially in the spirit of

obedience, even the new obedience of the gospel. My God! *release me from this bond!* and walking in the footsteps of the faith of our father Abraham, let me believe on Thee, not as a shield only, but as an exceeding great Reward also, who wills my sanctification, and rejoices over it, and finally Rewards it. Let this consideration have its direct and natural impulse on all the springs of activity within me; and cause me to go forth with confident alacrity in Thy service.—The controversy between faith and works has had a deadening effect on gospel obedience; and by relaxing the affinity between faith and a good conscience, we fear it may have led many, of their faith to make shipwreck. It has divided Christ, and broken up the entireness of his system of doctrine, so as to give men but a partial and *mutilated* view of it."—*Sabbath Readings: Genesis* xv.

the old Eutychian heresy—which the Westminster Divines have denounced, when they say that the Hypostatical union was effected without "conversion, composition, or confusion" of the two natures—many have, by one or other of the three perversions, or a combination of them, *dehumanized* Christ—especially in respect of his knowledge—deifying his human spirit with omniscience. Such persons will (I doubt not) object to my representation of the manner in which his soul was, both in youth and manhood, trained and lifted up to higher and higher states of intelligence, compared with previous states of acquirement. But the opposite notion is as absurd as it is anti-scriptural. All the great theologians of the Calvinistic school zealously controverted it. I have given a specimen of Turretin's exposure at page 232. Let Turretin and Dr. Dick, then, be disposed of before I am censured. But I repeat that my abolition of the popular enormity, on the subject of the Nature of the Cup of Gethsemane, is but little dependent on the dispelling of the Eutychian fantasy.

If to some it should appear that a denominational partiality has prevailed in selecting Testimonies to the Doctrine of the Reward of Grace, I assure them that my partiality for my *subject* was far too strong to prevent my refusing to adduce any witness, of whatever evangelical denomination, whom I knew to be favourable.

W. A.

Uddingston, Glasgow, *February, 1870.*

FILIAL HONOUR OF GOD.

"IF I BE A FATHER, WHERE IS MINE HONOUR?"
—*Malachi* i. 6.

How large and delightful a part of the Bible is spoiled for us by bad Kings!—not only marring its beauty and troubling the fountain of its consolation, but positively rendering it odious and hateful. When the peoples of Russia, France, Spain, Rome, and many others whom I might mention—almost all the peoples of the whole world, in fact, are told that God is a great King, how little is that calculated to recommend Him to their affection and confidence! From what they see in their kings, and experience of them, their associations with the name must be rather terror and abhorrence. Even here, at home, the name of a king has no warmth in it.— Blessed be God! that, through having raised up for us a noble ancestry for the constitutional bridling of royalty, He has so secured our liberties that the personal character of the sovereign does not greatly affect our interests; and that we have no reason, like many other despotically oppressed nations, to hate the title and image of a king. But we must travel back as far as

Alfred in England, and Bruce in Scotland, before we discover that paternity of character which makes royalty a fit image for illustrating the bounty and care of the Almighty. Not what kings are, but what kings should be, must be the recourse of our meditations, when reasoning upwards from what is mortal we would infer the excellence of God, and delight and comfort ourselves in the contemplation of his Majesty.

But let us be candid, brethren, and avoid partiality. There are others besides Kings who spoil the Bible for us, and hinder our appreciation of its mercy. Many Fathers do it. May there not be some one present who, not to speak of cruelty, yet, by his harshness, his moroseness, his perpetual fault-finding, and scolding, and taunting, and refusing or grudging the expense or trouble of the least gratification, incapacitates his child for perceiving anything precious in the testimony that God is a Father to his people? Ah! yes; there are some hardly used children who appreciate the great consolation. They accompanied home a school-fellow or playmate; and when they saw the kindness with which his father welcomed and cherished him, they reflected, This must be what the Bible means when it says, "Like as a father pitieth his children, so doth the Lord pity us." They learned abroad what they could never learn at home; they learned from seeing the happy experience of another what they could never learn from the miserable experience of themselves; they learned from another father's conduct what they could never learn from yours. So when they returned to your house, and were received with, or rather repulsed by your usual indifference or quarrelling, they said to themselves, We have seen to-day a different kind of father from our own; and from under your unamiable and spirit-crushing treatment, they lifted up their young hearts, and wiping away their tears, said, We have a *right* Father in heaven.—Ah! parents; the undutifulness of an ungrateful and disobedient child is bad; but that of a cold-hearted, sour-hearted father is greatly worse. Perhaps I may not say it is more unjust, but I am sure it is more unnatural. How it spoils the very best of the Bible for us! The wickedness of kings is nothing to it for evil influence.

But neither does the father himself escape the incapacitating influence. That man who does not feel any tenderness of heart for his child cannot derive much comfort for himself from those representations of the scripture in which God is set forth as a confidence in his paternal relation. They must be for him what the fifth petition of the Lord's prayer is for a revengeful man; for whom to pray, Forgive me my debts, as I forgive my debtors, is rather the imprecating of a curse on himself, than the importuning of a blessing. Similarly, how many parents, when in distress they are exhorted to confide in God's mercy because he is their Father, might well reply, If God do not pity us more than we have pitied our children, we have not much to expect!— Parents, love your children; cherish them; be at pains with them and expenses for them. Take care that according to the apostle's warning ye "provoke them not to anger, lest they be discouraged" (Colos. iii. 21; Ephes. vi. 4), by sacrificing their comfort or honour, either to mammon, or passion, or obduracy. Shame, fools! to be obdurate against your own flesh and blood. Forgive, restore to favour, and encourage them. The more you love and cherish them, the more easily will you believe and comprehend the affection with which the Eternal Father loves yourselves.—"Does God love me as tenderly as I love my child?" More tenderly far, whoever you may be who asks so foolish a question. Even a mother may forget; but God is the Father of mercies.

Before dismissing this topic, there may be need in some instances for a sentence of qualification of the preceding remarks. Brother and sister parents, let us distinguish carefully betwixt genuine kindness and cruel indulgence. He that spareth the rod in whatever form—of frown, rebuke, or corporal chastisement—hateth his child; and he who pampers his child and nurses his self-will, provides a fortune for him of poverty and manifold misery. We have more forbearance, perhaps, with the over-indulgent than with the harsh parent; his conduct is not so unnatural. But it is difficult to decide whether of the two modes of maltreatment has entailed more evil on the world. For my own part, I suspect that the desolation and loss produced by the heart-breaking, heart-crushing, and spirit-depressing process, especially when the cases of violent rebound are taken into calculation, have been more extensive and woeful. Others however will contend that over-indulgence is pregnant with more evil. It is needless to dispute on the subject. Let both be avoided. Both are of disastrous consequence. Tender but Faithful; and again, Faithful but Tender, let that be the motto of our parental training.

Who more spoil the Bible for us? Will any one determine for me whether bad Fathers or bad Children spoil more of it? Between them, what an impairing of its force and marring of its beauty they make, when it employs these two relations so extensively for the illustration and inculcation of its benignant and holy principles! We have already considered the case of bad fathers; let us now review that of bad sons, and of not a few bad daughters besides.

Were the honouring of parents the universal custom and order—did we never see anything in the manners of children but dutiful, filial respect, in referring to the fair moral scene, how strong our appeal would be on behalf of piety, when we reasoned, Let God receive the honour of a Father! But amid the abounding disrespect and disobedience, the appeal has lost almost the whole of its force. From the general state of the observance of duty towards parents on earth now-a-days, we can learn little of what is our duty towards our Father in heaven. In his days the apostle could hold this argument with the disciples—"We have had fathers of our flesh which corrected us, and we gave them reverence: shall we not much rather be in subjection unto the Father of spirits, and live?" (Heb. xii. 9.) How little of such reverence is to be discovered among us! How much of the very opposite! What petulance and impertinence, and gainsaying, and back-answering, and self-willed resistance, and imperious demandings, and sulkiness if refused! Yea, what mocking of parents! —for their deficiency in scholarship, for instance, by those who have acquired all that educational polish on which they presume, at the expense of those who have submitted to so much toil and self-denial, in gaining for their offspring those accomplishments which are now used by the base ingrates as weapons for their dishonour, and the breaking and stabbing of their hearts. "The eye that mocketh at his father, and [despiseth to obey his mother, the ravens of the valley shall pick it out, and the young eagles shall eat it." Just judgment of the righteous God!

Whatever may be said of the state of other departments of morals it is undeniable that we have suffered a sad degeneracy in this. When we read the account of heathen manners, in the Andria of Terence for instance, and compare them with our own, it looks as if Christianity had relaxed the bonds of filial duty. Even at the present day the testimony of my Israelitish friends is unanimous, that the duty is held far more sacred among the Jews than among us. And what is more humiliating—when the Rev. Tiyo Soga came to this country to be educated as a Missionary, a principal thing in our manners which astonished him was the deficiency of respect for parents, compared with the reverence which prevailed in the wilds of Caffraria. When I suggested that it might be the slavish submission of terror, he indignantly answered, No; that, notwithstanding polygamy, Caffre fathers showed great love for all their children; and that, in return, men who had grown up to warriors' estate, and had possessions and families of their own, continued to be as tenderly and scrupulously reverential of their fathers as when they were little children.

The defence of our faith is that it was not always with our morals and manners as it is now. About thirty years since, conversing with a lady of great intelligence and piety, above eighty years of age—so that her testimony for the state of matters reaches back to what it was about a century ago—after having detailed a number of particulars in which she thought the world had improved since she was young, when I said it was very pleasing and encouraging to be assured that we were making progress in the right direction, but that I suspected she might have a counter-balancing charge of declensions for humbling us,—" I *have that,*" said she, " and first and chief of all " (I thought it might be our high living, or fraudulent bankruptcies, or political and ecclesiastical contentions), " first and chief of all," she said, " the frightsome neglect and breaking of the fifth commandment: not to say mere children, there are many grown up youths of both sexes who though otherwise decent and well enough behaved, yet treat their parents with such impertinence and wilfulness as, in my young days, would have made them the talk of the whole parish, as being verily of the generation of the wicked Ham."

Nevertheless, there has been left to us a remnant of the devoted filial affection of the olden time—the delicious sight of which may assist us in forming a conception of the duty which we owe to our Father-God; it being always remembered that in consequence of the limitation of the rights of earthly parents, and the personal imperfections which a discerning child cannot but see in the best of them, there must, even in the case of the most dutifully disposed son or daughter, be a *reserve* in the submission, and a *suppression* in the reverence, for which there can be no apology nor excuse on the part of a child of God contemplating the perfection of that Heavenly Father to whom entire and unqualified honour is due.

I propose to illustrate this dutiful honour under these three heads—Confidence in his Love, Obedience to his Commandment, and Resignation under the Afflictive Dispensations of his Providence. The last of these, as we shall afterwards see, is a compound of the two others; but of such importance is it that I shall give it a special illustration by itself.

Confidence.

The first, as it is also the last, and the universally pervading principle of filial honour, is to *confide* in a father's love; and by nothing is he more dishonoured than by his child's regarding him with suspicion, and doubt of his affection. I say to thee, child, Suspect whom you may, distrust not your father. From whomsoever you may withhold the information, reveal your sorrow or difficulty to him, without fear that he will slight it or refuse his sympathy and help. And yet, woe's us again for these earthly fathers! What with the selfishness and unnaturalness of some of them, and the ignorance and unskilfulness of others of them, and the impotence of the whole of them for the redress of our worst grievances—how miserable, how orphanlike our condition would be had we no better Father! They! What is the use of telling them of many of our griefs? It would only pain them without our obtaining any benefit for ourselves. Tell me, then, brethren, if *you* honour God by rising in heart above every earthly confidence, and seeking repose for your spirits in his paternal love—whatever your sorrow may be, unbosoming yourselves of it to Him, in the assurance of finding his effectual sympathy? So far as confidence in the love is concerned, some of you would do this to your earthly parents, being persuaded that they would help you if they *could*. But God *can*. So that if you have no recourse to Him it must be because you suspect his *willingness*. How deeply, how criminally, you dishonour Him, by likening Him to some of those unnatural parents, already referred to, who are the monster-opprobrium of our race! Oh, take care that you insult not the paternal love of God! I would alarm you out of your alarm for Him. To be alarmed for God is your most offensive crime; whereas to rejoice confidingly in Him is your most acceptable service. Your pain is your sin; your pleasure is your duty. Trust Him, then, with all your sin, that his Fatherly mercy may forgive it. Trust Him with your unclean, and perverse, and dull heart, that He may wash it, and rectify it, and animate it—beautifying his child. Trust Him with your life, that He may preserve it; with your character, that He may defend it; with your studies, that He may enliven your powers; with your business, that He may prosper it; with your family, that He may make it flourish. Trust Him with your church, that He may revive, establish and honour it; as a patriot, trust Him with your country; as a philanthropist, trust Him with the world. Trust Him with all the desire and expectation of your heart, that He may consummate your happiness in the inheritance of his heavenly kingdom. Trust Him, and plead with Him, as He is your Father. Oh, call Him *that.* It is his most divine delight to hear you salute Him with the paternal name. "Wilt thou not cry unto Me, my Father?" is the expression of his yearning remonstrance. (Jer. iii. 4.) To gain it from thy heart He spared not the humiliation and death of his only begotten Son.

Let no one say that it is a Sabbath-school treatment of men to call upon them to give their hearts to God with child-like confidence. Though it were the assembled princes of this world, with the retinue of their nobles and most valiant warriors, their condition would truly be that of weak and ignorant children, needful of the help and guidance of the Divine Father. They are all dying and being hurried on to the judgment-seat in eternity. But that which especially interests us at present is, that it would be his divine gratification to act a father's part by them, if they would permit Him— yes, if they would but *permit* Him, and grant Him an opportunity. God is love; and, as I have just signified, to gain for Himself the paternal gratification He withheld not the greatest and most costly gift his infinite resources could bestow—his co-substantial Son, humiliated in incarnation, to be a member of the human family; that in consideration of his representative expiatory death for his guilty brethren—they in faith approving and accepting—it might be consistent with the rectitude and holiness of his government to take them back—kings and beggars, philosophers and publicans, to take them all back—for equally all are "his offspring"—to take them back to his house from which as prodigals they have wandered, that He may enjoy them—yes, *enjoy* them as a father enjoys his children. For of these two profitings—I speak of pleasure as a profit—that of a father who enjoys his child as an object on which he may lavish the endearments of his full heart, yearning for escape—and that of the child on whom the lavishment is poured forth, the profiting of the parent is by much the greater. And such is the profiting which the Eternal Father had in view by giving up his Son to humiliation and death. Woe! woe! to the impenitent prodigal, who obstinately remains in the wilderness among the swine, treating slightingly, yea scornfully, all invitations to return home; and refusing God the profiting of all his outlay and expenditure on the work of Redemption—the profiting of that joy which is in heaven over the recovery of a lost son.

OBEDIENCE.

When the first principle of filial honour, Confidence in God's love, is secured, the honouring of Him, which consists in Obedience, follows naturally and necessarily. —I read in books, and they tell me in conversation, that there once existed a species of mankind who seemed to enjoy the most undoubting confidence in God's love, as secured for them by the work of Christ, who were yet selfish, fraudulent, sensual, and extensively immoral in their conduct. Notwithstanding the respectability of those who make this report, I am incredulous of its truth. At all events, of this am I sure, that if any such characters exist among us now, they are exceedingly rare. I have never met with one, though my ministerial experience has been more extensive and intimate than that of many. I am not ignorant that some hold the *theory* of what is called Antinomianism; and I am grieved to be obliged to acknowledge that there is a great multitude who *profess to believe* evangelical doctrine in a good scriptural form, when yet their practice is impure; but the problem is, to produce an individual who exhibits unmistakeable symptoms that he delights himself confidingly in God's love, when he is yet either of immoral habits or even not characterized by a positive active virtue. I for one know not, and never knew such a man. Those that I know, of whom I am persuaded that they have an abiding joyous trust in God's paternal love, are all as obedient as they are confiding (I would that some were as confiding as they are obedient); and there is no preaching, I am persuaded, which makes such a waste of words as that which exerts itself in the exposure and rebuke of the man who indulges an antinomian confidence. It is a mere beating of the air—there is no one to represent the character. It is not only a moral, it is a kind of physical impossibility that a soul which has "entered into the holiest by the blood of Jesus" to hold filial intercourse with the Father of spirits, should fail of being transformed into the divine moral likeness: Beholding as in a glass the glory of the Lord, it is changed into the same image from glory to glory. (2 Cor. iii. 18.) I explain, however, that I do not censure, as vain, refutations of the antinomian *theory*. On the contrary, I often engage myself with them; but it is chiefly in the way of confuting the allegations of infidels or the priesthood of Rome, that a dogma so obnoxious is either contained in the Scripture or justly imputable to our Protestant doctrine of Justification by faith alone. It is testimonies against the *confidence* of immoral men which I regard as being vain. There is no such confidence existing to be reprobated; unless those evanescent feelings which I am about to notice be called improperly by that name.

There are sensations and emotions produced and excited at times, by adventitious circumstances, within the bosoms of those who are destitute of *principle*, which bear a resemblance to those which are the fruits of faith;—when, as affected by the music of the psalm, or the eloquence of the sermon, or the pathos of the funeral prayer, they shall be the subjects of feelings akin to the devout experience of the saints; and thence conclude, that "after all they are not so very bad, and that at bottom there is something good in them: why should they fear?" For evincing the spuriousness of all such merely emotional sensations there is the infallible test, "If ye love Me, keep my commandments;"—not a selection of them only, according to humour or natural temperament or convenience, but the whole of them—prescriptive and prohibitive, in thought, word, deed, and gesture;—nor occasionally and fitfully only, but at all times, regularly and constantly;—and over all, with alacrity and zeal.

Principles of Obedience.

Besides that influence already noticed to which the children of God are passively subjected, so as by the great principle of Imitation to be transformed into a likeness of the divine Holiness, there are chiefly four considerations which make them studious of keeping his commandments.

Consideration First. In grateful return for all his bounty, they are eager to *do* and studious to *be* what will please and gratify Him: for such views have they of God, that although He be the Eternal and Self-Sufficient One, they believe of Him that He is not only interested in their happiness and well-being, but that He takes pleasure in their moral fairness and well-doing. If He delight in the growing and blooming of the lilies of the field, they reflect, How much more must He not delight in the scene of the growing and blooming of the graces of his children? Let us therefore grow and bloom, they say, that He may have some gratification in us, in acknowledgment of all his love. So they cultivate their minds in devout and benevolent affections, and engage in such work as they know from his Law will delight Him; and as they work they sing; and when they see his approving smile, how it animates them! how honoured they feel! This is the highest inspiration of virtue. It needs such conceptions of God's fatherliness and *moral sensibilities* as are rare. It needs a study of the Incarnation, in which God is manifested and made somewhat comprehensible to us, as acting in the guise and through the medium of our own nature. "He that hath seen me," says Christ, "hath seen the Father." Let us therefore observe and study Christ as portrayed in the gospels; and when we see with what complacency, delight, and richness of benediction He salutes all with whom He meets who observe the divine commandment, let us infer and calculate that the same is the estimation in which the Eternal Father holds them, since Christ is set forth to exemplify Him.

Consideration Second. The second consideration by which God's children are influenced in their obedience, is that of the manner in which his Honour, in the estimation of others, is concerned in it. This motive is not perhaps so elevated and refined as the former, but it is of great power. A well-disposed son is more tender and jealous of his father's honour than of his own. In the case of the children of God the feeling induces them to engage in such work as will persuade others to honour Him; but especially to be careful lest either by such conduct as is impure and perverse, or by such as is wanting in honour and generosity, they might do Him any discredit, as the father of an unworthy family. Whose child are you?—you who are so low-bornlike in your ways, so foul-mouthed because so foul-hearted, if not foul in deeds, in your stories, and jestings, and songs and toasts of double-meaning, with all your impish, small-devil leering and winking—whose child are you, sir, I ask? And whose are you?—you with the spiteful tongue because you have a venomous heart, swollen with pride and envy and malice and all uncharitableness?—and you with the niggard hand because your heart is so small?—and you with the deceitful tongue and trickish hand with its pen because you have the heart of a knave?—one and all of you, and all you like them, whose children are you? Say not that you are God's, nor presume to associate with them at his table, lest it induce people to blaspheme God as the Father of such a vile family. It would verily be an eating and drinking of damnation.

Many and not a few poor children suffer in character and estimation by the unworthiness of their fathers; but there is a sad balancing of the account by the manner in which many and not a few unhappy fathers suffer discredit by the unworthiness of their children. The children of God are alive and awake to this danger, and are keenly sensitive on the point of his honour lest it should sustain any damage through *them*. Even from lawful enjoyments they will abstain, when in the eyes of neighbours their participation would have the appearance of evil; and they will increase their charities above what is strictly dutiful, so as to straiten themselves and their families; not from the fear of themselves suffering in character, but to prevent those who are ignorant of their circumstances from imputing to their Father's treatment of them a want of care in training them to generosity.

Consideration Third.—The third reason wherefore God's children are diligent and scrupulous in their obedience is the lowest and rudest; but, alas for the weakness of our principles! generally the most needful and potent. Though Christian faith removes the terror of a *Judge's punishment* of rebellion (vindicatory of the righteousness of the government, by a believing contemplation of the Lamb of God, who substitutionarily burdened Himself with our guilt and bore its *penalty,* so as to effect for us reconciliation to the divine government, and recovery to the family of God), yet the same faith substitutes in the place of the former terror salutary fear of a *Father's chastisement*—for the amendment of his children who may err—in vindication of the honour of his family, and as an expression of his displeasure with sin, wherever and in whomsoever his offended holiness may see it. When in the treatment of believers in his Son, restored to his family, God lays aside the Sword of Justice, He assumes the Rod of Correction. The distinction is as important as it is obvious. He who does not receive it must, at best, have but clouded views of the scheme of Christian salvation: but he who apprehends it approvingly has not much more to learn which is vitally important.* Be advised and warned, then, some of you. It needs not that I threaten your declension, and your love growing cool, and your worldliness waxing warm, and your circumspection relaxing, and your conscience blunting— it needs not that I threaten any one of you, that as an apostate God will disown you as a child of his, and erase your name from his Testament,—the Book of Life—so as to cut you off from any inheritance of his

---

* Throughout the decrees and canons of the Council of Trent the idea does not once occur of the afflictions of the saints being of the nature of Fatherly chastisements. They are all represented as being Judicial punishments to be escaped from, or reduced and finally exhausted, by the satisfaction of penance and indulgences and masses and purgatorial torments. The virulence of all this blasphemy appears more strikingly when we reflect that the Institutes of Calvin had already been published; than whom no one, even till the present day, has written more clearly, cogently, and impressively on the distinction betwixt punishments and chastisements, both with proofs from the Scripture and illustrations from the Fathers.—(See *Institutes, Book iii., Chap. 4.*) It must be acknowledged, however, that the Westminster Divines are less explicit on the subject than might have been expected, as will be shown afterwards.

heavenly kingdom,—it needs nothing so extreme and frightful as this to persuade you by the terrors of the Lord: There are those *chastisements*. Oh, God's Fatherly chastisements! they are sometimes heavier and more exquisitely painful than the Judicial punishments of this world's tyrants; and there is *that* in the idea of them fitted to make some of us quake for fear, and calling for instant repentance and resolutions and vows of amendment, lest that uplifted Rod should quickly smite. And there is enough in it to make even the most circumspect among us stricter than ever in their watching against temptations to indolence, formality, and perverseness of whatever character.

And yet, this is not all. There is God's *frown;* yea, the hiding of his face; so that all joy in Him is for a season quenched in horrid darkness. There is a prevailing misconception on this subject. It is most true that God never chastises any of his children without having a merciful respect to their own advantage and profit, so that they may be made partakers of his holiness. (Heb. xii. 10.) But many misinterpret this, so as greatly to diminish the force of the lesson. They imagine and teach, that in correcting his erring child God acts only as a wise physician does, in administering to his patient a nauseous or drastic medicine, or subjecting him to a painful operation. This is a great mistake. God's chastisements are not only regulated by a regard to his children's profiting, but are *sharpened* by a holy indignation against sin, and a design to vindicate the violated honour of Himself and his family.

In proportion as He is merciful is He jealous of his honour. The best of earthly fathers are distinguished by this union of kindness and self-respect. Let us be wary then. By a faithful continuance in well-doing let us study to please Him, so as to avoid both the Correction of his rod and the Frown of his anger.

Consideration Fourth.—The children of God are animated in their obedience and well-doing, unless their faith be censurably incomplete, by the prospect of being richly *rewarded.*

I have come to a point in these illustrations, the treatment of which will not give me the slightest difficulty, doctrinally; but which, on the contrary, appears so plain to me rationally, morally, and scripturally, that all my difficulty will lie in preserving due moderation in the censure and exposure of such as oppose or ignore it. Even with all my precaution against exceeding legitimate bounds, my testimony must assume somewhat of the character of a *manifesto* against a great wrong done to the honour of God, the integrity of the gospel, and the character and comfort of the Church. And should any expression which I use appear in way of protest too strong, or in way of mockery too bitter, let my friends reflect how great is the evil, how urgent the demand for its removal, and how, from its inveteracy, no gentle handling can be of any avail for the end.

The principal points of my argument are these:— *First,* That though no ostensibly good works of unregenerated men are of any avail for their eternal happiness, yet, to those who have obtained remission of their sins, and re-instatement as children in the divine family, through faith in the redeeming work of Christ, God makes promise that He will recompense their own works of filial obedience with rewards proportioned to their respective degrees of diligence and zeal, in the distribution of the honours and stations (" places ") of the inheritance of the heavenly kingdom. *Second*, That this promise of Reward is made with an explicitness and pervading recurrence such as are not exceeded in the case of any other subject of revelation. *Third*, That it is not only lawful for God's children to animate themselves in the discharge of their duty with this promise, but that it is a despite done to his truth and parental love to show insensibility to its encouragement. *Fourth*, That an unbelieving failure of apprehending the promise is greatly prejudicial to the cause of holiness, through withholding that which is designed by the Lord to be a principal incitement to pious exertion. *Fifth*, That all preaching, how much soever it may magnify the work of Christ, in which the promised reward to the work of his saints is not systematically displayed for their encouragement, is at best the preaching of a *mutilated* gospel. *Sixth*, That any preaching in which the doctrine is reprobated under the allegation that it is impure legalism, and adversative to the scheme of salvation by Grace, convicts the preacher, first, of his having profanely fancied some scheme of salvation of his own, since the divine scheme, according to a multitude of declarations of Scripture, contains the arrangement; and, secondly, of his being grammatically incompetent. The term *grace* signifies favour or bounty: and is it not very bountiful that a saint's own good works, being such as they are, should be acknowledged with a reward? This is as much of the nature of Grace as that at first he should have been justified by faith and admitted to a place in the family. *Seventh*, That instead of the scheme of salvation being marred in its attribute of Grace, as some presume to say it would have been, by the Rewardableness of the saint's own works receiving a place in it, on the contrary, such marring would have appeared if it had been denied a place—inasmuch as it is *ungracious* for a father not to reward the obedience of a faithful and dutiful son. Accordingly an apostle says, " God is not unrighteous to forget your work and labour of love."* (Heb. vi. 10.) *Eighth*, That so far as the opinions of the most eminent Reformers and the Confessions of the chief Churches of the Reformation are admitted to be a rule of judgment, those preachers who do not entertain and proclaim the doctrine of the reward of the good works of the saints are evinced to be defectively *non-orthodox*, on a subject

---

* The common interpretation is that the "unrighteousness," the idea of which is here reprobated, consists in the non-fulfilment of a promise. This is nearly sufficient for my purpose. But it is inferential and circuitous. And I am persuaded that unrighteousness is imputed to forgetfulness directly, irrespectively of any promise, in the sense of its being unseemly, and wanting in that *moral propriety* according to which a father acknowledges and rewards the obedience of his children. The word of the original seems to admit of this meaning of defect of graciousness, as distinguished from the perversity of injustice.

OBEDIENCE.

of great importance; and those who denounce it are convicted of being flagrantly *heretical*. When they impute heresy to those who hold and teach it, *ipso facto* they themselves incur the charge of the misdemeanour.—As for myself, I make no account—not the smallest—of those testimonies of uninspired men, as possessing *authority* for the determination of my faith; but since so many render them the homage, I take advantage of their prejudice for convincing them of error and persuading them of truth. In an Appendix I will furnish a selection of such testimonies; and meantime I satisfy myself with producing that of the Westminster Divines, occurring chap. xvi., sec. 6, of their Confession:—"The *persons* of believers, being accepted through Christ, their *good works* also are accepted in Him—not as though they were in this life unblameable and unreprovable in God's sight, but that He, looking upon them in his Son, is pleased [by way of grace] to *accept* and *reward* that which is sincere, although accompanied with many weaknesses and imperfections." It is also noteworthy that in their Larger Catechism, at Quest. 45, "rewarding their obedience" stands in the enumeration of Christ's kingly acts in the government of his people.

Such is the substance of my affirmation and contention. But I do not intend to discuss the various propositions formally and in their order. In the course, however, of the following discursive treatment of the subject, each will be found, at one turn or another, to have received illustration and practical enforcement.

At the outset, then, assuming for a moment as granted, that the state of the scriptural evidence on the subject is such as I have represented it to be, I appeal, If it be not something wonderful, that in what is called the Evangelical community—the only class (comprehending all who confess the expiatory death of Christ and the sanctifying agency of the Holy Ghost) in whom I feel fraternal interest—I appeal, I say, If it be not surpassingly wonderful, that there is not one in a hundred of its thousands of pulpits from which there ever proceeds the faintest whisper of the divine promise, for the excitement of the hearers to work and distribute with zeal and liberality, under the assurance that they will be amply rewarded for it all, by being advanced to stations nearer the throne than those which are assigned to such as, though members of the divine family, are yet comparatively sluggish and niggardly in their conduct? How rarely is such a whisper to be heard! Whisper, indeed! when even the singular few who give utterance to the promise do it so fitfully, so briefly, and with such apologetical explanations—verily whispering it.—Few, if any, will deny that this is, upon the whole, a truthful representation; and many, instead of resenting it as false or exaggerated, will contend that it is creditable to the Evangelical party that it is true, as evincing how well purged they are of the foulness of the doctrine of legal self-righteousness.

Hear, then, the Gospel (Matthew, chap. xix. ver. 27): "Then answered Peter, and said unto Him, Behold *we* have forsaken all, and followed Thee; what shall *we* have therefore?" What explanation do the zealots* give of this, consistently with their fancied scheme of Free Grace? Attend: The foolish and presumptuous question of the apostle, say they, was asked when he was in the infantile state of his faith, with much of the unclean spirit of legalism remaining yet to be purged out of him.—Nor is this sort of interpretation perpetrated only by vulgar declaimers. Archbishop Trench, in his Notes on the Parables (No. ix.), annotates thus: "In that question of Peter's, What shall we have? there spake out something of the spirit of the hireling."

Such, according to the verdict of the zealots, with his Lordship, the Primate, for their spokesman, being the corrupt state of Peter's principles, what was the medicine which Christ administered for purging him— a favourite mode of expression with them—of his hireling-spirit legalism?

Verse 28th, "And Jesus said unto them, Verily I say unto you, That ye who have followed Me, in the Regeneration, when the Son of Man shall sit in the throne of his glory, ye also shall sit upon twelve thrones, judging the twelve tribes of Israel." This was compensation promised especially to the Apostles; but they had their

---

* The designation is not happy, for intentionally it includes a number who are destitute even of zeal "without knowledge," and whose fierce denunciations of others are instigated merely by innate or sectarian rancour. Zealots, however, is the most convenient term I can find for briefly expressing the whole company of those who vilify that great doctrine of Grace, that God complacently regards the good works of his children with the purpose of rewarding them.

part also, in common with others, in what is subjoined:
—Ver. 29th, "And every one that hath forsaken houses, or brethren, or sisters, or father, or mother, or wife, or children, or lands, for My name's sake, shall receive an hundred fold [of compensation in one form or another], and shall inherit everlasting life."

Does not this appear to be a strange prescription for purging a man's heart of legalism and hireling mercenariness, if thereby is meant the expectation which he may entertain that, as a disciple of Christ, his heavenly Father will reward him well for all his labour, and self-denial, and endurance, in the [course of his filial obedience? Instead of its being a drastic purgative for expelling the expectation, simple people, who have not been to college to have themselves purged of common sense, might think it was rather like a cup of new wine for cherishing the expectation and exciting it into rapture.—It is all a vulgar mistake, says the Archbishop. See you not *the bitter* which the skilled physician, discerning the hireling spirit of his patient, mingles into the potion? Verse 30th, "But many that are first shall be last; and the last shall be first." He admits that, in answer to the mercenary question, Christ could not but allow that there would be great glory ultimately bestowed on the faithful, according to the scheme of Free Grace, and which, as a sequent, though not a consequence of their well-doing, may in a certain sense be called a reward; but that had He stopt short here it would have been as "fuel to the fire" (as the annotator expresses it) of the questioner's evil disposition. That He therefore adds the antidote, "many that are first shall be last;" by which He *warns Peter* that he shall be one of the last in the judgment day, if he go on indulging that hireling spirit of his, bewrayed by his question. Moreover, that for the more impressive teaching of this minatory lesson, He proceeds to give forth the parable, at the beginning of chapter xx., in which the guilty apostle is exhibited as a type of that party of labourers who entered the vineyard early in the morning, and were rebuked with such indignation for their murmuring, when, at hire-paying in the evening, they did not receive more than those who had wrought but one hour.

Such is the annotating of the learned, spiritual Dignitary. I denounce it all as being as fanciful and fantastic as it is odious—odious for the manner in which it calumniates a saint for whom nothing was so natural as that he should inquire, what would be the ultimate advantage of all these privations to which he was subjected in the faithful following of his Master—odious for the manner in which it imputes a severity to our Lord in the treatment of his disciples—even to mocking of their sacrifices and losses—so unlike Him, even when there were grounds for censure, of which here there were none. I, therefore, turn away in the meantime * from what is so offensive, to a quarter in which we find refreshment of heart in having Christ's pro-

---

* I will return to the exposure in a note in the Appendix, in connection with the illustration, that the parable of the labourers does not contain evidence that all saints shall be equally rewarded.

mise illustrated in Christ's spirit, by one who could appreciate with particular relish the cup of wine, as having been persecuted by that spurious Apostolical succession, so notorious for its mercenariness, in which the defamer of Peter, as being of a hireling spirit, holds a pre-eminent position, and who was recently so strenuous in asserting the claims of himself and his brotherhood for retaining that which the whole nation has denounced, with imperial voice, to be a hire of injustice. Hear, then, part of Matthew Henry's commentary on Christ's answer to Peter's question—

Verse 29th. " Losses for Christ are here supposed, and a recompense of these losses is secured. Thousands have dealt with Christ, and have trusted Him far; but never any one lost by Him; never any one but was an unspeakable gainer by Him when the account came to be balanced. Christ here gives his word for it, that He will not only indemnify his suffering servants, but will abundantly reward them. Let them make a schedule of their losses for Christ, and they shall be sure to receive an hundredfold. Cent. per cent. is great profit; what then is a hundred to one?"—Let the whole commentary be read. It is conceived in the famous author's happiest vein. Was Matthew Henry, too, then, I ask, a corrupter of the Gospel, calculating in a hireling spirit the profits of good works? Undoubtedly, in this instance at least, many of the zealots for a purely purged doctrine of Free Grace will say— themselves being purged of all grammar and honesty in the interpretation of much of the plainest testimony of the Word of God.

I suspend, however, for a little my *manifesto* against their perversions till I have distinctly and clearly erected the standard for adjudication.

Many feel a difficulty in attempting to reconcile these two doctrines: the one, that a sinner can be justified or pardoned and re-instated in the Divine family only through faith—laying hold on and pleading Christ's substitutionary work and obedience unto death on his behalf; and the other, that after he is thus justified his own good works are accepted and will be rewarded. Wherein is there even at first sight an apparent contrariety betwixt these two doctrines, even for a mind of feeble intelligence, if it would exercise a little thought? Instead of being mutually contradictory, the second is a most reasonable, almost necessary, consequent or complement of the first. The reward of a believer's own works proceeds from his being justified for Christ's work. By that justification he has been transferred from a rebel's position with a rebel's heart, where his works increased his condemnation, to a son's position with a son's heart where his works are pleasing to his Father. This distinction, or rather connection of the two doctrines is expressed, as I have already quoted (p. 23), by the Westminster Divines thus: "The *persons* of believers being *accepted* through Christ, their *good works* also are *accepted* in Him."*

Attend now more particularly to the *Reward*, for

---

* The expression occurs in the Augsburg Confession, and was adopted by all the Divines and Churches of the Reformation.—*(See Appendix.)*

which they give their testimony, as well as the *Acceptance*. Can any moral distinction be more easily discerned and comprehended than that of the Reward of Merit or Debt, and the Reward of Grace or Bounty? —the one, of Merit, being that with which a Master, according to equitable law, recompenses the labour of a hired servant; the other, of Grace, that with which a Father, without being obligated by law, and merely of good will, recompenses the labour of a son;—the one, *wages;* the other, any favour whatever, but especially a *share* of the *inheritance*. Now, the first species of Reward, that of Merit, is sternly denied a place in the system of Christian Salvation, except where Christ, mediatorially his Father's servant (Isaiah xlii. 1,) is rewarded with personal honour, and the gratification of the salvation of his brethren; but the second species, that of Grace, obtains wide scope in the recompense of believers. Here, then, is the order and connection: Believers in Christ are through his redeeming work restored from their prodigal and disowned condition to the position of sons and daughters in the family of God; as occupying which position they are indeed well certified and warned that should any perversity, or naughtiness, or remissness in duty presume to manifest itself it will subject them to *chastisement;* but not less well certified for their encouragement, that if they prove obedient, diligent, and zealous they shall be bountifully rewarded—each according to the degree and measure of his or her faithfulness—in the distribution of the honours and felicities of the inheritance of the heavenly kingdom.—Can anything be plainer than this, more consistent as a scheme, more reasonable as an arrangement of moral propriety, but especially more clearly Scriptural? And I remonstrate: How this dishonour of God, that the Threatening of his chastisement for disobedience obtains so much, often slave-like trembling credit, but the Promise of his reward so little or none at all?

This moral phenomenon in the Church, the almost universal want of being animated in well-doing, or sustained in patience by any expectation of being rewarded for it, when yet the promise of it pervades the Scripture as a first principle of its system of salvation—this phenomenon, I say, for it is truly of this class of wonders, needs some explanation of its cause, that we may understand how to attempt the removal of the evil.

Observe what it is *precisely* of which I complain. Were I to assert that in the evangelical discipleship there is discoverable but little expectation of a future heavenly felicity which sustains the heart under labours, privations, and afflictions of various name, I would be justly chargeable with the utterance not only of a calumny but an absurdity. It would be an excommunication of the whole Church; for there can be no faith where there is not such hope. I not only admit but zealously contend that among evangelical professors the consolation abounds. I boast of it; and with the exhibition of it challenge the sceptic and heretic to show us the like of it for happiness, and patient endurance under hard duty, or under heavy afflictions in the course of the pilgrimage of this life.—But here is my complaint and accusation :—That the vast majority—after contemplating in prospect the heavenly inheritance as being for God's redeemed children, universally, a region of felicity, admission within the precincts of which is secured for them by the meritorious work of Christ—should stop short here, satisfying themselves with the general expectation, and in neglect, amounting to a kind of despite of God's promise, refuse to proceed with calculating the manner in which their own works specially, after Christ's work for all in common, will affect their comparative degree of glory, and be distinctively rewarded with higher elevation and dignity amid the principalities of the kingdom, closer intimacy with Christ, and an advanced nearness to the throne of God, according to the superior excellence and abounding of their well-doing.* Hence all their works are performed only from a conscientious sense of duty, or from a feeling of gratitude, or in fear of being chastised for indolence, without the animating calculation—that if to the one pound of a dutiful, commendable, convenient subscription, sufficient for maintaining their *status* in the family, there be added another of self-denying, self-incommoding charity, then will God their Father,

* I protest against being misunderstood, as if I complained of there being a want of *competition* for honours. But I could not find a better way of expressing the idea of being actuated by the desire of standing *near the throne*.

who well-pleased beholds their work of love, make record of it for rewarding them with a degree of advancement in his heavenly kingdom.

Did foul legalism ever express itself with more presumptuous effrontery? Yea, it is worse than legalism—it is Popery entire, in its doctrine of works of Supererogation: So some will exclaim, who are as ignorant of the Protestantism of Calvin, as of the Popery of Pius IV. There is not a sentiment of what I have said to be found in the whole body of the decrees and canons of Trent, sanctioned by Pius. The doctrine of his Holiness is, that the martyrs, and such great saints as St. Dominic, famous for killing heretics, having wrought out more merit than is sufficient for their own necessities, the overplus is collected into the treasury of the church, whereof the Pope holds the key, to be dispensed by indulgences for the benefit of criminals or defaulters; "since" (the representation is Calvin's) "it would be incompatible with the justice of God to leave the overplus barren or unfruitful." Of course Calvin mocks at this doctrine of Pius, but what is *that* in it which excites his mockery? It is not the idea of there being in a hundred-fold fruitfulness a superabundance above what is necessary for a subordinate place of glory in the kingdom; since sixty-fold, yea thirty-fold is commended and accepted. That which provokes the sneer of the Reformer is the perplexity of his Holiness about what is to be done with the overplus of thirty in the sixty-fold case, and such a quantity as seventy in the hundred-fold case—

a perplexity which set him on contriving and fabricating the treasury chest for the help of those who are in arrears, "as if," says Calvin, "God did not know how to *augment* the glory of his servants according to the extent of his gifts,"* meaning thereby those gifts of spiritual influence in the strength of which they work. With the same view he says at another place,† "God is equally liberal in assigning a reward to good works as imparting ability to perform them." This argument is a favourite one with Calvin, and will afterwards afford us good help; but meantime I would fix the attention on the opinion of this great theologian and Reformer, pronounced so expressly: *first*, that the good works of believers will be *rewarded;* and, *secondly*, that the reward will be *augmented* according to the increase of the well-doing. That is exactly what I said, when the zealots exclaimed against my representation of the one pound more of self-denying charity gaining for the donors a degree of advancement in the heavenly kingdom—exclaimed against it, that it was impure legalism and Popish supererogation. I exclaim, in my turn, How contemptibly ignorant they are of Reformation doctrine! and How heretical they be as impugners of that great doctrine of grace, that the Lord will reward those works which his own grace has influenced! And when even the Pope has the moral sense to see that there is a superabundance in a hundred-fold above the sufficiency of thirty-fold, and is concerned that it be

* Institutes, B. iii., c. 5, sec. 3.   † c. xvi., sec. 2.

not lost, they denounce the whole—both the hundred-fold and thirty-fold—as being a mass of *filthy rags*, and claim to be regarded as specially zealous in defence of the doctrines of free grace—their own zeal, too, being of course only a filthy rag, for which they take no credit; for your zealot is notably meek and humble. This defaming of the righteousness of the saints, as being only of the character of filthy rags, will afterwards receive its castigation. Meantime I proceed with the argument.

It signifies little what either Pope Pius or Presbyter Calvin either approbates or reprobates. To the law and the testimony is the only appeal for determination. Here then is the testimony in the present instance: Luke xix. 12-26. He who improved the pound with which he was entrusted into five, was, on the King's return, rewarded with the honour of the administration of five cities; when he who had used more diligence, so as to improve his into ten, was advanced to the administration of ten cities. Have I said anything worse than that, I appeal to *you* who are so zealous for doctrine purged of all legalism ? Well, try your cathartic skill in having the gospel purged of that parable. Every verse of it is full of what you call the poison of legalism and popery. And the same is the state with hundreds of passages besides, disseminated throughout the Bible, enunciated on Divine authority by historians, prophets, psalmists, proverbialists, apostles, and most especially by Christ Himself speaking personally, as reported by evangelists. By the time your expurgation is completed you will have made an unsightly skeleton of the Book, and reduced it to very convenient dimensions for indolent hypocrisy. What mean you, I demand, when you are so vehement in your testifying that Christ's personal work avails everything, and that the work of his saints avails nothing in determining their position in the heavenly kingdom? Taking an illustrative case, Do you mean that in that day the Righteous Judge will bestow on the Penitent Thief and the Apostle Paul crowns of exactly equal dignity and splendour? The redeemed thief's crown will indeed be a peculiarly glorious one. His testimony for Christ, both of itself and in the circumstances, was of a very high order of faith. He has not received sufficient credit for it. Christ's cause has profited by it immensely; and in the day of manifestation he will be rewarded for it munificently. Though his course of well-doing was very short, yet God's good child as he was, just recovered to his Father's house, he made the best of his time. His soul ran a long way in the path of righteousness those few minutes that his poor mangled feet were transfixed to the cross. Nevertheless, even you, with all your pretentious orthodoxy, howsoever violatory of common sense, will scarcely, I imagine, plead that the crown of righteousness bestowed on him will equal in glory that with which Paul will be honoured. Yet whence any difference? Christ's work was the same, and the same equally for both. We are all agreed about that (both those who contend and those who deny that the sacrifice of

Christ was limited in its aspect), since the reclaimed thief is as patently demonstrated one of the election as is Paul. Whence then, I insist, the difference in the degrees of their future glory? There is but one honest and reasonable answer. Since *Christ's work* was the same for both, the difference in glory must arise from difference in their *own works* respectively. A good child of God though the penitent thief was, Paul was a better; and, as a reward of his superior well doing, will receive a larger share of the inheritance.

Besides that party, however, whose pretensions and perverseness I have been exposing, there are humble believers who in perplexity object, How can there be anything of heavenly glory gained by our own good works, when yet Christ is declared to be "All, and in all" to his people (Colos. iii. 11.) It is melancholy to find in private intercourse how much even intelligent Christians will, at times, perplex and mystify themselves, and occasion themselves errors and delusions,— not to speak of making themselves very ridiculous—by quoting, as proof, words of Scripture in a sense and with an application in which they were never used by the sacred writers—a simple reference to whom, with a reading of the context, would dissolve all the fancy. In the present instance the phrase, as employed by the apostle, signifies that in the Church there is no recognised distinction betwixt Greek and Jew, circumcision and uncircumcision, barbarian, Scythian, bond and free, but that Christ is *All* as the central engrossing object of the holy fellowship, and *in all*, as pervading all with his influence, assimilating them to Himself, and uniting them one to another. Nevertheless the words may be very widely *accommodated* to other subjects. In the contemplations of the saint Christ appears *in all things* whatever, as being connected with them in one relation or another; and He is *All* to him as a Helper. In a multitude of cases He is more than that, and performs the whole of the work Himself. But in the case of our duty—the one now before us—He does not execute for us the commanded work of praise and prayer, and charity and patience, &c., but only *helps* us to do it. And yet such is the extent of the help that with but little use of a figure He may be represented as performing the whole of the work.

I should think that those good brethren who are tender of Christ's honour, and who shrank from my representations of their own works being rewarded, in a manner independently of Him, will feel that I am now coming round to their satisfaction. Let me complete the satisfaction: Who gained for you that position which you occupy as recovered sons and daughters of God, and but for whom you would never have had an opportunity to do any filial work to be rewarded? Who perpetuates your standing in the Family, either by his Intercession for you, that you be not ejected, or by his influences of persuasion and threatening, and discipline, as Steward of the House, saves you from turning prodigal again, when tempted by the remains of the evil passions of the flesh and spirit? Who furnishes you with materials for your work, money for your charities, and learning for your pleadings for truth and righteousness? Who instructs you in your work and superintends you in its execution, so that it is good and acceptable work? Who gives you strength for it? Who gives you heart for it?—To all these and similar interrogatories is not the answer one and the same, Christ, and Christ alone? What are you in *status* or position—what in qualification for working—for which you are not indebted to Him? (1 Cor. iv. 7; Phil. ii. 13.) Why, as God's *workmanship*, you are said to be "*created* in Christ Jesus unto good works" (Ephes. ii. 10), so that the works are properly rather his than yours—his by authorship, yours only by agency. Paul, when defending his apostleship, having braved his revilers with the fact that he had laboured more abundantly than all the other apostles, immediately adds, "Yet not I, but the grace of God which was with me." (1 Cor. xv. 10.) And we all know that Paul found this enabling and operating grace of God as gained for him by Christ, and deposited with Christ for distribution. (Heb. xiii. 21.) So is it with you: all your good works are the product of grace communicated by Christ; so that neither the credit nor merit belongs to yourselves. "Agreed, agreed!" you will say, "we are quite satisfied with you now." But I am not yet satisfied with you. The good work excogitated by your minds and executed by your hands being admitted by you to be rather Christ's work than yours, see how you dishonour Him and derogate from his glory when you dis-esteem that work as being of no valuable and rewardable consideration, notwithstanding all the care and watchfulness which He expends in producing it out of you. It is your silly selves and your ignorant spiritual directors who are the legalists, estimating the work produced by Christ's Spirit as if it were some law-work of Pharisees. Shame on you, brethren! Assert your prerogative as an agency for Christ—as members of that mystical body of which He is Head—for producing work well-pleasing to his Father; and for the reward of which HE waits according to the terms of the Covenant of Redemption. And what is the reward He expects—of all other enjoyments the most gratifying to Him? It is the rewarding of those members of his mystical body through whose agency He has produced the work. When on earth He prayed on behalf of his faithful followers—"Father, *I will* that they also, whom Thou hast given Me, be with Me where I am; that they may behold My glory, which Thou hast given Me." (John xvii. 24.) Such is a specimen of the request—eminent divines have not scrupled in calling it the mediatorial *claim*—which in That day He will prefer on behalf of yourselves: so that when you receive your crowns you will, in the first instance, cast them at his feet, saying "All the merit is Thine!" But He will replace them on your heads, that for eternity you may wear them.

Having thus explained distinctly what my complaint is against the evangelical profession of the present day,

I proceed to an examination of the causes of the phenomenon, that, when the promise of God is so express, and so abundantly repeated, that He will reward the good works of his recovered believing children, there should yet be found so few who are animated by it in their well-doing, or sustained by it under their tribulations, so that patience have its perfect work.

First, then, and principally, a cause is the deficient teaching of the ministers of the gospel, some of whom are ignorant of the distinction, howsoever old and obvious, of the Rewards of Merit and of Grace; others of whom, though they are acquaint with it, yet fear that the people would not comprehend it, and pervert to presumptuous ends of self-righteousness the preaching of the latter, as if it were a preaching of the former; and it is not a few of them only who are restrained by fear of the zealots, who might *report* them as being *unsound*. Hence their preaching is engrossed by denunciations of the Meritoriousness of good works, to the exclusion of any recommendation of them as being Rewardable; and so as to enforce them only as evidence of the genuineness of a profession of the faith which justifies. In these circumstances the idea of working and spending in prospect of a reward never enters the heads of the people; and should the imagination of it for a moment insinuate itself into their hearts, under the reading of any of the frequently recurring testimonies of the scripture, they instantly expel it as a temptation of the Wicked One. What is the remedy for all this most mischievous anti-scriptural absurdity?

It is the people with whom, as a preacher, I have especially to deal. But were it a company of brethren in the ministry of the gospel whom I addressed—overlooking the two other parties whom I have distinguished—I would remonstrate with those who acknowledge the truth of the doctrine, but plead in defence of their *ignoring* it in their ministrations, that they fear ignorance might abuse it to self-righteous ends, to the injury of the doctrine of salvation by free grace through faith in the cross of Christ. Supposing there were some danger of this, Would not the proper course be to proclaim the truth, with a guarding of it from perversion? But against your ignoring and suppression of it, I protest, as a most unreasonable and unequitable sacrificing of the rights comfort and animation in duty of the *children* in fear—of what?—of inducing *aliens* to become good workers on erroneous principles! Think of that!—that you should abstain from preaching the Reward of good works for the encouragement of the pious John, lest it should influence the worldly James to commence donations to the poor, and subscriptions to the Bible Society, in the expectation that he would thereby merit salvation! Well, what although he should? What would be the harm of it? The poor and the Bible Society would rather profit by it; and although unworthy James would not be a gainer, neither would he be spiritually a loser, for he was before as bad as may be; whereas by your deficient preaching you defraud worthy John of his rights, concealing from him much of what his Father has bequeathed to him in his Testament, the knowledge of which would benefit him greatly; and all this on the pretext that were you to tell the whole truth it might injure his unbelieving neighbour, by setting him to work for the relief of the poor on legal principles! How considerate you are of the interests of aliens at the expense of the defrauded children!

And yet, when the interests of the children are sacrificed, are those of the aliens promoted? On the contrary, there is no fear so groundless as the apprehension that the preaching of the Saint's Reward would generate and cherish a spirit of self-righteousness. Let it be preached as the Scripture teaches it. It requires but little guarding. Let it be preached as the Reward of Grace of the works of those, but of those only, who have been constituted God's children through faith in Christ's atonement—then, when the saints receive the encouragement to which they are entitled, formalists will be constrained to reflect, if these works and observances with which they endeavour to pacify their consciences have that justifying faith for their parentage; and if they be animated by the spirit of Adoption. There is nothing better fitted to reach the heart with convincing and converting influence than the preaching of the Reward of Works thus qualified. Let such preaching then abound, that the Spirit may have an opportunity to apply it with power. Viewing the subject generally: When so many of the brethren are ready to say, in the bitterness of their spirits, that it would be preposterous for them to begin to preach to their people, for their encouragement, the Reward of good works, since there are no good works among them to be rewarded, let them reflect, if the deficiency of their ministry, in this respect, be not a principal reason of the barrenness of which they complain. Whatever be the cause, let them do their duty, and preach an entire unmutilated gospel. They have no right to complain of the people's indolence so long as they withhold from them that which God has prepared so abundantly, and commanded to be administered to them as a principal stimulant of duty. The Hope of Reward is indeed subordinate, but subordinate only to Gratitude, and needful as a complement to Gratitude to fill up the measure of Christian motive to a vigorous, generous, patient well-doing.

I have already signified, however, that it is rather the people than ministers with whom I have to deal in these popular illustrations. What then should the people do for rectifying the evil which the phenomenon complained of presents, and which is ascribable to such an extent to the deficient ministrations of the pulpit? I answer, principally, that they should be less popish and more protestant in spirit than a great multitude of them are—less servile in forming their opinions, and more independent and self-reliant—asserting more strenuously their own priesthood, and resenting all priestly claims of subjection made on them by others —thankful for the *help* of pastors, but treating with scorn all airs and pretensions of *lordship* over faith and conscience—listening attentively and respectfully to those pastors' teachings, but claiming liberty to try them by the great Standard, and to refuse them credit if they do not find them, according to their own judgment, answering the measure—deferring, in some cases, to their superior scholarship, but contending that there are many things so plain that their own common sense is as competent to form a correct judgment as the most erudite learning; for example, that these words (occurring at 2 Cor. ix. 6), "He which soweth sparingly shall reap also sparingly; and he which soweth bountifully shall reap also bountifully," signify not only that a believer's good work shall be *rewarded* (even the "sparingly" declares that), but that the better the work is the greater shall be the reward—that this is a judgment which the humblest ploughman is as qualified to form, and as much entitled to form for himself, as the learnedest scholar. The same is the case with a great multitude of similar plain declarations and provisions of the universal Father's Testament.

This is only the old lesson, some will say, with which we are all familiar, of the Right of Private Judgment, which none but the impostors and the thralls of popery question. But though the lesson is old, yet every succeeding generation must be taught it anew, and though it is one of very easy intellectual comprehension, it is of very difficult practice, and rarely practised well. The great bulk of Protestants have arrived at the belief of what they profess precisely in the same way in which Papists have proceeded. It has not been by an application to the Divine oracle to hear directly for themselves, either in the way of being discoverers of the truth, or in the way of having the instructions of their friends tested or verified. I do not accuse them of being wanting in sincerity in making their profession, nor even of believing primarily on the mere authority of man. Even the Papists and Tractarians are not so bad as that. My charge is, that what they believe to be of divine authority they believe, not because they themselves have consulted the Inspired Testimony and found it there, but because books and ministers have reported to them that such are its contents. Their faith, therefore, rests only on *secondhand*, hearsay, fallible evidence. Now, that a multitude of those who are converted have attained to saving Faith in this way, I doubt not. It was the only way possible for the great majority in the churches at the Reformation, when they neither had Bibles nor were able to read them, though they had possessed them. It is the only way for not a few among ourselves whose education was neglected in their youth, as well as for those who dwell in barbarous lands into which the Gospel has been newly introduced. And, though moral responsibility commences much earlier, the faith of youthful piety under ten, or even under twelve years of age, is mostly of this traditional character. But that grown up men and women, possessed of clearly printed Bibles, able to read them, and who may do so without fear of an Inquisitor's visit, and some of whom boast of their intellectual culture, and claim and take liberty to judge for themselves in all other matters—that such persons should have recourse to the traditionary way of being saved is at once highly sinful, deeply disgraceful, thoroughly popish, dangerous, and at best meagre in salvation, compared with that faith which is acquired by a personal consultation of the oracle, to hear God's own voice declaring his will.

At first thoughts, concerning so much as it does both "nobility" (Acts xvii. 11) and satisfaction, it may appear strange that so few should exercise this right of Private Judgment. But there is nothing which is more easily explained. Observe what is precisely the fault. Though there is exhibited among us not a little anti-protestant, pro-popery devotion, in an ecclesiastical way, at least (it is to be hoped not in the way of personal conviction, for the lamentable exhibition which it would make of the miserable state of some men's intellect, and their moral and political principles as well), devotion in an ecclesiastical way to the Articles, and Confessions, and Catechisms, and Prayer Books of men dead hundreds of years ago, yet there is not much observable among us of *reverence* for a *living clergy*, as the divinely authorised, infallible interpreters of God's Word. But there exists and abounds what is akin to it, and nearly as prejudicial—and with no generation in Scotland, since the Reformation, did it abound more than with the present—that natural popery—the tap-root of formal popery—which, from aversion of the heart to exercise the mind on God and things spiritual and eternal, endeavours to escape from the distasteful trouble, and devolves on a priesthood, of one kind or another, the task and responsibility of determining a Faith for them, "cut and dry," though it should be a bundle of tares and thistles. There is nothing more in demand by the great multitude—most especially fashionables—lords and their ladies, and wealthy merchants and their dressed up wives and daughters—than "religion made easy," by getting others to *settle divinity* for them.

The *second* cause of the phenomenon, that when the scripture is so replenished with the encouragement to work, by the promise of a reward, there should be so few who are animated by it, is still more melancholy than that which has been explained, very melancholy though it be. It is, that so many of our self-denominated and church-received *communicated* Christians are of such a character that it is not easy, in many cases not possible, either for themselves howsoever self-complacent, or their neighbours howsoever charitable, to conceive of their being *rewarded* for anything they do. By their decency, their integrity in business, small charities necessary to keep character, and courtesy of manners, they may save themselves from the accusation of a decided belying of their Sabbath day and sacramental profession; but it defies imagination to think of some of them being *rewarded* with the distinction of the administration even of the smallest village, when the King returns to acknowledge the services of those who, during his absence, have been faithful to his cause. And they themselves are so conscious of the want of ever making any rewardable exertion, or expenditure of either time, labour, money or thought, and much less any self-sacrifice of pleasure or of worldly name and honour for religion's sake, that they do not expect any reward. It would be utterly preposterous to do so. The thing to be rewarded does not exist. The blessing wants an object on which it may be pronounced. They would be quite satisfied and at ease if they were only sure that they shall be admitted into the kingdom at all, though it should be to inhabit the lowliest cottage in the most retired corner, the furthest away from the Throne. They have no ambition after nearness to that. Just let them *in*, and do not shut them out to the darkness, where there is nothing but weeping and wailing and gnashing of teeth. That is all they wish when they take a religious fit under a storm at sea, or when attacked by a sharp threatening disease. I would be more at ease about myself than I am, as a candidate for heavenly honours, were I chargeable with no other sin than that of a slanderous libelling and caricaturing of the visible church, when I maintain and testify that I have given a veritable, and that, too, a very lenient description of fully one half of our communicated Christians, comprehending not a few of the zealot class, who vaunt of their purged orthodoxy. We shall see. The day of purgation of character and principles draws nigh. The signs of it flash luridly over all the firmaments—civil and ecclesiastical, moral and mercantile.* The Lord has taken the fan into his

---

* Luke xxi. 25-27. "And there shall be signs in the sun, and in the

hand, and He will thoroughly purge his floor. *Hoist the drum! A tempest down from God!* "Behold the whirlwind of the Lord goeth forth with fury, a continuing whirlwind; it shall fall with pain upon the head of the wicked. The fierce anger of the Lord shall not return, until He have done it, and until He have performed the intents of his heart. Thus saith the Lord of Hosts, Behold evil shall go forth from nation to nation, and a great whirlwind shall be raised up from the coasts of the earth. And the slain of the Lord shall be at that day from one end of the earth even unto the other end of the earth. *In the latter days ye shall consider it.*" (Jer. xxx. 23; xxv. 32; xxiii. 20.)

Do not our days appear to be the latter days? And meantime, during the respite from the threatened storm, when we consult for the safety of all, let us be especially earnest for the interests of those lamentable *formalists* with whom we have such intimate connections. First, by prayerful invocation bringing down on them the power of that Spirit who "convinces of sin;" needful for the conversion of all, but especially for arousing out of torpor decent-living, hypocrised, self-deceiving, communicated professors. What a scaly, hard, tough, thick, leviathan hide must be penetrated before the hearts of such be reached! Those of harlots

moon, and in the stars [of government]; and [down] upon the earth [among the subjects] distress of nations, with perplexity; the sea and the waves [of the populations] *roaring;* men's hearts failing them for fear, and for looking after those things which are coming on the earth: for the powers of heaven shall be shaken. And then . . . . "—Read the scripture and see what follows.

and publicans, Christ says, are of easier conquest. (Matt. xxi. 31.) Nothing but the lightning bolts of God's Spirit can effect it. But, as constituted fellow-workers with God, in his employing of human agency, and electrifying our weak words and making thunder-bolts of them, let us earnestly, with wise adaptation, always affectionately, but sometimes, like Christ, scornfully of their pretensions, warn these men and women, that, notwithstanding all their decencies, and proprieties, and sacraments, and attendance on an evangelical ministry, and reception and enrolment as church members, it is questionable if, at best, they shall gain even that bare admission within the precincts of the kingdom of God, which is all they aspire to, when the religious fit is on them through fear of dying; that it requires a stretch of charity to hope it of them; that it is difficult to find even the briefest clause in the whole of the Testamentary deed of the Heavenly Father, which, according to the most "benign interpretation," secures for them even a hut in a nook of His kingdom; and that they must *think* more, and *believe* more, and *feel* more, and *work* a great deal more, and in causes of piety and benevolence *spend* much more—in a word, show *earnestness*—earnestness Godward, Christward, churchward, poorward, selfward—in respect of what is truly self, the immortal *soul*, before there be any hope, which is not delusive, even of that shelter in a hut in a nook. But the hut and nook is all a fancy, and a poor enough one too, forced on me as an illustration by the character of those who would be glad for the banishment, as a commutation for capital punishment. It is all a fancy, I say. There is no such thing in the kingdom of God. All stand before the Throne. (Rev. vii. 9),—some nearer and higher up on the Hill of God, in the ascending circles of the principalities and powers, but all, under the blaze of glory which shines down from the mountain top of Presence, and uniting in the universal chorus of praise. And depend upon it —it is common sense, though there were no scripture for it—that in order to receive a place, even in the lowest, I should say the least elevated, circle at the bottom of that Hill of God, there must be something excellent in character and conduct, which makes it morally fit and proper that any one should obtain the position, when others who want the qualification are denied it. In other words, there must be moral qualification, on which the Reward of Grace may be bestowed, in the distribution of that heavenly inheritance which Christ has *merited* for his people. And according to the degree of qualification—in strong faith, lively feeling, busy working, liberal giving, and patient endurance of afflictions, shall be the magnitude of the share awarded and rewarded. Ho! for the display of the righteousness of the Righteous Judge in that day! when those who are now first, in the world's estimation, yea the church's, shall be made last; and those that are last shall be made first; and when those who are made last shall be the first to acknowledge, now that their moral sense is disabused of all worldly sophistications, that the award is right, when the last are preferred before them; and that they themselves are the recipients of great mercy when admitted to the position, though an inferior one, which has been assigned them. Well, if admitted to the kingdom at all, of course you will then be satisfied with your position. But what feel you *now*, lady proud, *in the prospect*, that, unless you mend your manners, that pious waiting maid, whose life you weary out by servile attendance, and whose feelings you so frequently injure by your pettish and contemptuous reproaches, will shine in a circle high above you on the mount of God? Your rectified judgment will approve of the arrangement; but the *prospect*, I should think, cannot be very agreeable. Mend your manners, then, or your downcome is certain. And please—speak a warning word to the squire, your husband, about his treatment of the pious footman, lest he (the squire I mean) fall into the same condemnation. Preserve the order of nature, in spite of the Tempter who so often prevails to violate it, that the first in privilege in this world be the first in station in the next.

The *third* cause of the phenomenon calling at present for an explanation, is the miscalculation of genuine modesty and humility—promoted (I mean the miscalculation) by preachers, who are ever confessing in prayers and denouncing in sermons all the righteousness of the Church as being but as "filthy rags." These very prayers, then, and all the psalm-singing, and sacramental and other observances of Sabbath, and contributions to the poor, and Sabbath-class keeping, and home instruction of children, &c., &c., must be only a presentation to the Lord of "filthy rags." What a worship of Him! Can He accept of it? What wonder is there that the poor people never imagine they will be *rewarded* for it?—There is no greater perversion of the words of scripture, amid the much that is perpetrated, than the misapplication of these words of the Prophet. When he uses them (Isaiah lxiv. 6), he is engaged in denouncing the pretentious piety of ritualistic, apostate Israel. How accurately prepared the expression is for all the *surplice* and altar-cloth and other rag-worship of Rome and her Anglican brood! But even making great allowance for that force of formalism of expression, by which much of what is called our extemporaneous praying is characterised, it is astonishing how extensively that old barbarism maintains its ground, of the pulpit confessing in the name of the whole church that in the way of righteousness they produce nothing but filthy rags. The question is not about what in their state of nature they once were, and their inability in that state to work out their own salvation, which may be humbly confessed in such language appropriately: but that any one, acting as the organ of a church's devotions, should employ the expression in reference to their present condition, is an abuse of the liberty of his office, and an insult offered to the character of the church, if it be worthy of a church's name. Can intelligent piety blame me for being over-severe in exposing to reprobation this great scandal? Are there not cause enough and room enough for confession and bewailing of "weaknesses and imperfections," as the Westminster divines express it, existing and abounding in the church, without praying and preaching as if it contained nothing but infidelity and reprobacy, needful of conversion;—so that grateful piety never enjoys that expression of its feelings, "by the grace of God I am what I am;" and, which is worse, so that formality is lulled into deeper false security, pleading, in answer to any remonstrances of conscience, that *decency* is enough; since the minister confesses for us one and all in a mass, that we are only respectable hypocrites—the works of the most highly reputed among us being only as filthy rags.

Hear now the Gospel, in contradiction of what is so profane and absurd: Philippians iv. 18. The church at Philippi had sent Paul, when a prisoner at Rome, a donation for the supply of his necessities. It could not in the circumstances have been great. But whatever it may have been, mark how Paul expresses himself when acknowledging its receipt. "I am full, having received of Epaphroditus the things which were sent from you, *an odour of a sweet smell, a sacrifice acceptable, well-pleasing to God.*" Something very different *that* from the "filthy rags" which the superlatively pure contenders for the doctrines of free grace represent all works whatsoever, of all men whomsoever, to be. What is their attempted explanation? Just something superlatively absurd. It is that the works of the Philippians were intrinsically, that is in their own nature, and as they came from their hearts and hands, naught but filthy rags; but that Christ took them, and by his intercession incensed (fumigated) them, and out of his own active obedience supplemented them, and made them up into entire fabrics of fine linen, clean and white. Such is the vaunted orthodoxy of some preachers, admired by the ignorant *as the real gospel.* It would not be worth while to answer the jumble of nonsense, but for the opportunity which it affords of illustrating the truth.

First, then, it unhappily cannot be denied that there occasionally occur even among believers acts of seeming well-doing, which from defect of genuine motive are of the character of filthy rags. But Christ does not convert them into fine linen. He covers them, and buries them out of sight; by his intercession having obtained their pardon.

Secondly, I contend that the works of the Philippians were intrinsically good—good of themselves, without any extrinsic incensing or supplementing of them by Christ; for the plain reason that they were primarily produced by Christ Himself—by the influence of his own Spirit. I admit that there *may have been* mixed with the fine linen of the Spirit a few rags of carnal policy; but I contend that what Paul calls an "acceptable sacrifice" must have consisted mainly of fine linen; and that when the rags, if any, were abstracted, it was in itself, *intrinsically,* "well-pleasing" to the Lord.

But when I have admitted the possibility of there being a small proportion of rags in the sacrifice of the Philippians, no one is warranted to say that *certainly* there was; and I feel that I act somewhat ungenerously by those eminent saints in admitting to their defamers the possibility. Does not the exuberant description of the Apostle demand for them the credit of having offered a sacrifice without spot or blemish? And I denounce the man as profanely presumptuous who, in the face of the apostolic testimonial, may say they were necessarily tainted and defective. Though it were admitted—an admission which many refuse to make—that a state of sinless perfection, like that of Adam before his fall, is unattainable in this world—that though commanded as a duty (Matt. v. 48) it is not designed that the Spirit should effect such a complete moral recovery for any one in this mortal state—though this, I say, were admitted by all, yet it would not imply that *every act* of a regenerated man's life was tainted and defective, and that in no instance he performed his duty unblameably. Paul says, "Pray for us: for we trust we have a good conscience, in all things willing to live honestly." (Heb. xiii. 18.) Was Paul the only person whom the Spirit has enabled to keep a good conscience? On the contrary, I assert that there is a multitude among ourselves who, although "in many things they offend,"* yet also in many things are conscious of acting with integrity of heart towards both God and man. It would be monstrous were it otherwise. And he who mocks at the

---

* James iii. 2. "In many things we offend all." In the original the word translated *offend* signifies *stumbling*, which at Rom. xi. 11, is distinguished from *falling*. At present, however, I make nothing of this; it is sufficient for my purpose that the apostle does not affirm that all Christians are in every thing they do guilty of sin.

consciousness of integrity as the complacence of self-deceivers, not only violates candour, but defames the work of the Spirit; and, moreover, gives good grounds for suspecting himself, as being a person of such low character, that from his own experience he cannot comprehend how others should be sincere and generous. Attend: I am well persuaded that Lydia's contribution to that "sacrifice" of the church at Philippi was as pure an act of righteousness as any one which Adam in his state of innocence ever performed. And the cause of such a statement appearing to many, as no doubt it will, paradoxical or worse, is the low condition of our so-called evangelical preaching, dealing almost exclusively in grimness about the degeneracy produced by the Fall, and so little in animation about the moral recovery to a life of rewardable righteousness, effected by the great Redemption. Mark, however, the specialty of my expression: It is, that I am *well persuaded* of the equal excellence of Lydia's work. In regard of Adam, I am *convinced* that every act of his before his fall was perfect in holiness; that is a kind of truism. But in regard of Lydia, though I am *convinced*, too, that it is quite *possible* she offered her sacrifice with a perfect heart, so that there was not a shred of rag in it, yet I am only *persuaded* that she actually did so—persuaded of it as a *high probability*—persuaded of it by her personal excellence, but especially by Paul's characterising of her donation as "an odour of a sweet smell, a sacrifice acceptable, well-pleasing to God." Reflect, *that* is not merely Paul's opinion, expressed in a grateful mood—

as one inspired he is reporting the judgment of God. Instead of my claim for the work of Lydia (and there have been and are many ladies just as good as she), that it equalled in excellence any act of Adam in his innocence, being an extravagant claim, let me inform those who are not versed in dogmatical theology, that eminent divines have maintained that it is possible for the saints to attain to a more elevated holiness than that reached by Adam; because they enjoy in Christ a Spiritual aid which, they say, was not vouchsafed to him. But when they say so, I think they err; for I hold that Adam in innocence was sustained by Spiritual aid; so that all the privilege enjoyed by Lydia consisted in *that* being restored to her in Christ which was lost in Adam.* I, therefore, claim for her only equality in holiness.

Thirdly, Though the works of the Philippians have been demonstrated to be intrinsically good and acceptable, this does not prove them to be *meritorious*, but only *fit* for a reward should grace choose;—that is, so far as the works are considered as having been performed by the Philippians. According to the parable (Luke xvii. 7-10), they were " unprofitable servants, " not by any means in the sense of the filthy-rag school of prophets that they were "useless;"—on the contrary, the parable shews they were serviceable to the master; but in the sense that they had only "done that which was their duty to do," in consideration of what they had

---

* See author's Treatise on Regeneration, p. 49.

already received, so as to have no claim on a reward after the work was done. But when these works are taken account of in another way, according to a former illustration (p. 39)—as in origin influenced by Christ, and in their execution superintended by Him, so that the Philippians were only the agents of works which were properly his, then does their meritoriousness become conspicuous; when, as the Steward of the family, He presents them before his Father's throne, pleading with a kind of exultation their excellence and beauty, as gained by Him out of his once miserable brethren—thus *incensing* them, and waiting for the reward, according to the terms of the covenant, renewing the memorable plea, "Father, I will."

These illustrations of the Philippians' *sacrifice* of good works have prepared the way for a practical dealing with those whose objection induced them—those whose humility and modesty, independently of doctrinal sophistications, make them shrink from the idea of any thing they may do obtaining a reward. There are especially three ways in which such persons miscalculate, some in one or other of the ways, others in two, or the whole of them.

First,—Some say that though they were convinced of the truth of the doctrine that good works shall be graciously rewarded, yet it would yield them no satisfaction; since, notwithstanding the abundance of their seeming well-doing, they yet question if they ever produce one work which is not defective, if not in quantity, at least in quality—in its *motivity*, or the spirit by which it is actuated:—that they suspect there is always in that motivity a mixture of selfish and carnal considerations, and that it is never purely spiritual; so that it is impossible for them to expect any reward for that which is so tainted in its origin. I answer: In such reflections there is not only oft-times the influence of a morbid self-jealousy, but an ignorant miscalculation of what is genuine motive; calling that evil which is not only constitutionally necessary and legitimate, but which is cherished by the Spirit of Holiness. For example: We frequently find friends deploring that they were actuated in their well-doing partly by passion —by an emotion of anger; as if it were sinful to be angry in any case and in whatever degree; whereas, there are many instances in which the sin lies in not being angry, or only moderately excited. But I forego this plea. Admitted that, with pious and generous considerations, there was in the motivity of your act the mixture of an impure element, must this characterize the whole of the work, even though it should be the smaller element, and that, too, in the estimation of a Father, judging of the work of his child? I had an earthly father —I know now—of a heart tremulously concerned about my welfare, but, according to a foolish notion prevailing in those days, systematically austere, in fear he might injure me by appearing to be well pleased! But his austerity was sweetness compared with what your imagination imputes to the Father of Mercies.

When of the two rows of *hoeing* prescribed, one might be executed insufficiently, in my haste to join playmates, he would rebuke me sharply, and warn me about the future; but referring to the other, he would say, That is tolerably well done: you may now pull a few berries; and there is a penny to buy more line for your kite. The ignorant may mock, but the parable is pregnant, and I press its application.

When the subscription sheet for the widow and her fatherless children was presented to you, on reading the preamble, you felt that a pound was even more than your fair proportion of charity; but you resolved to give it. On glancing, however, over the list of subscribers your eye lighted on the name of a competitor in trade, across the street, who had subscribed two; and after a little reflection you resolved to be equal with him, and subscribed accordingly. Now I can easily conceive of that additional pound being subscribed in a rewardable spirit; so that without deduction the whole of your subscription has been entered to your credit in the heavenly ledger. You may have reflected that the unfavourable comparison which neighbours, ignorant of circumstances, would make of your one pound with his two, would diminish your influence, which you are conscious is salutary, in the church and community at large, and increase his, which you are convinced is prejudicial. If that was your motive, your act was one of self-denial in the cause of righteousness—as good as any missionary subscription—and could not fail of being accepted and entered for reward. But suppose your motive for the subscription of that additional pound was merely to save your *custom* from some withdrawment of dealers with you, and the transference of it to your rival—Well, there would not be anything *perverse* in that; it would be a prudent and legitimate calculation in conducting your business. It might even be spiritually commendable; if your rule, for instance, were to consecrate a tithe of your profits to the Lord, and you reflected that that tithe was threatened with diminution—an evil which you took means to prevent. But I drop this consideration; and assuming that it was merely a prudent, self-defensive act—though diligence in business is a scripturally commanded good work, yet I do not, in this instance, claim any heavenly reward for it. I hope it will have all you expect—the reward in this world with which the providence of our Heavenly Father usually prospers the prudence and industry of his children. Let that second pound go then; sink it in the calculation. But what though you should? Will it drag into oblivion with it the first, contributed so genuinely in the fear of God, and the love of the widow and the fatherless? When you have *hoed* the first row so well, do you think no consideration is made of it because there is deficiency in the *hoeing* of the second, and that, too, when it was not *prescribed* to you? Is that the way with *your* Father in heaven? It was not the way with mine on earth, though the reverse of an over-indulgent one. And as my warrant for making the comparison, hear Christ, who knows our Heavenly Father intimately:

"If ye then, *though* evil, know how to give good gifts unto your children, how much more shall your Father which is in heaven give good things to them that ask Him?" I add, how much more still to them that *work well* for them? I have his own authority for the addition: "If ye forgive men their trespasses, your Heavenly Father will also forgive you."

I may not, however, through partiality for my subject, suppress the other part of the oracle. Suppose you subscribed that additional pound spitefully—in revenge for some slight or affront which your rival put on you—that under the guise of pity of the widow you took advantage of the opportunity, and designed to mortify him, and reduce him in public estimation, when with means known to be much greater than yours his contribution was only equal; if this was your design, then hear your doom. "If ye forgive not men their trespasses, neither will your Father forgive your trespasses." There are only two ways now in which your double-pound subscription may be dealt with: either that the maliciousness of the second be made to counterbalance and neutralise the generosity of the first, so that the whole of the subscription will be simply lost money; or, that you be credited with the generosity for a reward, but debited with the maliciousness for a sharp stroke of chastisement. You might prefer the former way, but I incline to the opinion that the latter is the mode of *entry* in the books. Haste you, then, and repent; the chastisement impends. Commit your case to the Great Intercessor, that He may get this bad

OBEDIENCE.

business adjusted for you. He will not convert that truly filthy rag of the malicious bank note into fine linen. That exceeds his power, great though it be. All He can do is to get it buried out of sight. He will plead that He has died for your pardon; that you are sorry and ashamed for what you have done, and are resolved and promise that you will never do the like again. There now: the nasty thing is out of the way, and your golden pound shines, without obstruction, with its promise of a reward.

All this the zealots will, of course, regard with the uttermost scorn, or actual shuddering for its more than common impure legalism. But, besides them, there will, no doubt, be others who, taking credit to themselves for being persons of common sense, though not skilled theologians, regard my representations as being very fanciful, if not fantastic. It is because both of the parties are so very ignorant that they feel and talk in this way. The greater shame to the zealots, with their orthodox pretensions. The Westminster Divines, as formerly quoted at page 23, to which I refer, declare explicitly and clearly for the principle I have been illustrating. These words, "pleased to accept and reward *that which is sincere*," contain their decision on the first *good* pound of my illustration; the words, "although accompanied with many weaknesses and imperfections," contain a reference to the second *bad* pound, which they hide away in a much more tender way than I do, and less strictly orthodox, as I shall presently show.—But first, I instance another orthodox utterance. Hear Father Calvin: "The imperfection which universally (?) deforms even the good works of the faithful, being *buried in oblivion,* their works are accounted righteous, or, which is the same thing, are imputed for righteousness." (Institutes, B. iii., c. xvii., sec. 8.) I am little ambitious of either being or appearing original; but in the present instance, for showing that I have pondered the subject, and thoughtfully elaborated its principles, and not merely made up fanciful stories for the popular ear, in words used loosely and inconsiderately, I feel I am entitled to assert my independency by stating that, long before I consulted the Institutes, I had arrived at that conclusion respecting the faults and imperfections of the works of the saints, for which I selected as the most fitting expression, that they are "buried out of sight," leaving conspicuous only what is good for acceptance and reward, while Calvin uses the expression "buried in oblivion," leaving what is good to be "accounted righteous," or "imputed for righteousness." Who will mock when I felicitate myself, not only on the sameness of views, but the coincidence of the expressions of them?

Nevertheless, just as I have intimated that there is a deficiency in the statement of the Westminster Divines, so I find fault with that of Calvin; inasmuch as neither of the parties adverts to the *chastisement,* unless there be speedy repentance, which will overtake the faults, under Paternal Administration, though "buried out of sight," in the eye of Regal Justice, so as to be exempt from *punishment.* It is true that Calvin, under another

OBEDIENCE. 67

topic, illustrates very strikingly how the avenging temporal *punishments* of the law have been converted by the Gospel into salutary *chastisements*. (B. iii., c. iv., sec. 35.) But to prevent misconception he should have reproduced and interwoven the distinction, when representing the imperfections of the faithful as being "buried in oblivion." No person of intelligence can read his otherwise admirable exposition of the Reward of the good works of the saints, without feeling the defect. Is no notice, then, taken in any way of our sins? must be the frequently recurring reflection of any one who is not conversant with the whole of his system.— The Westminster Divines are subject to the same censure. When stating that God is "pleased to accept and reward that which is sincere" in the conduct of the saints, "although accompanied with many weaknesses and imperfections," the vindication of the moral system of the Gospel required a qualifying clause, remanding these imperfections to paternal chastisements; and especially when their Confession is elsewhere little adapted to form and establish in the mind one of the most important distinctions of the Gospel—afflictions judicially *punitive*, and afflictions paternally *corrective*. Throughout the Confession the distinction is not categorically made. It may only be inferred from a short phrase in chapter twelfth, in which " chastened by Him as a Father" occurs in the enumeration of the privileges of adoption. In chapter seventeenth, those who succumb to temptation are said to " bring temporal judgments on themselves," a form of expression which scarcely even insinuates *chastisement*. In the Larger Catechism, "correcting them for their sins" occurs in the enumeration of Christ's acts as a king, in the government of his people; but that is all. In the Shorter Catechism, neither the word chastisement, nor the idea of it is discoverable. How strange it is that this should be the whole of what these Evangelical Standards, as they are called, contain on a subject of such importance! But having indicated the deficiency, and how it is to be supplied, I return from the censure to enrich my page with the re-transcription of their invaluable deliverance, notwithstanding its defect: "The *persons* of believers being accepted through Christ, their *good works* also are accepted in Him; not as though they were in this life wholly unblameable and unreprovable in God's sight; but that He, looking upon them in his Son, IS PLEASED TO ACCEPT AND REWARD THAT WHICH IS SINCERE, although accompanied with many weaknesses and imperfections"—[*which weaknesses and imperfections are under the covert of Christ's atonement* judicially "*buried out of sight, in oblivion*," *to be dealt with in the way of* paternal *discipline and correction*]. These words in brackets are my proposed amendment of the Confession!

Second.—The next reason wherefore humble modesty takes no encouragement from the promise of its work being rewarded, is its miscalculation of the measure according to which God estimates the work. The poor widow who has given away her two mites, and after that can do nothing for the weary disciple, but give him a cup of cold water, cannot understand how the great God, with all his goodness, can reward anything so small and insignificant. Nay, Nay, she says, All my reward depends on Christ's work for me, and on nothing that I myself may do. But although she cannot understand this, she should believe it implicitly, since God makes a promise of it, to fail of being animated by which is indicative rather of unbelief than of modesty. I will help her faith, however, to be explicit, by showing her the reason of the matter.

1st, then, let her understand and reflect that, although in the distribution of the rewards of Grace there is a proportion observed betwixt the degrees of *good spirit* in which the different works are performed, and the degrees of excellence in the reward, yet is there no proportion in respect of the material or mercantile value of the works and rewards; as when the labour of the reaper is equivalent in value to his wages. This is the *ratio* of the Reward of Merit, according to which the work and the reward are in point of worth reciprocal. But, as has been largely illustrated, this law has no place in the scheme of Christian Salvation. The Reward at large is a Father's inheritance to be distributed to the children in its palaces and principalities of different degrees of honour; not certainly because any of them have given work and service for their shares of equivalent value, but according to the manner in which they have approved themselves to be of *good spirit*, as children *worthy*—worthy of their Father (1 Thess. ii. 10), *qualified* for administration in that kingdom of holiness—a *goodness of spirit* which according to circumstances may be manifested as well by small works as by those of larger bulk: "For if there be first a willing mind, it is accepted according to that a man hath, and not according to that he hath not." (2 Cor. viii. 12.)

There is one of Christ's parables strikingly illustrative of this principle which many indiscriminatingly confound with that which has been already employed in our argument (p. 35), as if the two were parallel; whereas they are counterparts of one another, supplying one another's deficiencies, and requiring to be studied together in order to our obtaining a complete view of the doctrine of the Reward of Grace. In the one, the Parable of the Pounds (Luke xix. 12-26), all the servants received the same amount of capital or stock, and started with equal privileges; but they differed in respect of diligence in "occupying" their pounds; and one of them who by trading increased his into ten, was on his Lord's return rewarded with the honour of the principality of ten cities; and another who had increased his only into five, was indeed graciously received, but comparatively with coolness in the salutation, and advanced to the principality of only five cities. But in the other parable of the Talents (Matt. xxv. 14-23), the capitals with which the various servants were entrusted were different; while two were equally diligent in their trading. The first doubled his original capital, but not less did the second double his. What then was the reception with which they met respectively when their Lord returned to reckon with them? Behold the equity! Equal diligence, equally rewarded! To the first, when he presented himself with his five talents increased twofold, He said—

Well done, good and faithful servant; thou hast been faithful over a few things, I will make thee ruler over many things: enter thou into the Joy of thy Lord.*

Then turning to the other who presented himself with his two talents equally increased twofold, He said unto him—

Well done, good and faithful servant; thou hast been faithful over a few things, I will make thee ruler over many things: enter thou into the Joy of thy Lord.

Word for word; benediction for benediction; an equal principality of power; a seat of equal honour at the Royal Banquet. It is all most refreshing for the moral sense. The Parable is the poor man's charter. It proclaims to him, Do your *proportion*, and you will be made equal with the greatest of them in the day of the righteous judgment of God. Yea, exert yourself a little more: make two talents *five*, and you will be glorified above them all, unless they

---

* The word *Hara*, translated *Joy*, denotes the Banqueting Hall in which the King entertained the Princes of his empire. (Burder's O.C., 1000.) At Luke xxii. 30, we find a similar union of feasting and ruling.

too exert themselves additionally and proportionally. So, you who are wealthy, be ye advised too. There may be a *respectable* "occupying" of your advantages with which you are deluding yourselves. Your five talents, increased only the length of eight or nine, will insure your inferiority in the distribution of the honours of the kingdom. Nay, to be safe, you must carry forward the "trading" in works of piety and benevolence to the threefold accumulation, lest some menial kitchen maid and plodding ploughman, with only a Sabbath-school's education, should, by the manner in which they "occupy" the pittance of wages you give them, in supporting their aged parents, and contributing their monthly sixpences to the Missionary Society, outshine you in the day when God will be Judge, by whose rule of judgment many who are first in this world shall be made last in the next, and *vice versa*. This was with Christ at once a frequent warning and frequent encouragement, and in imitation of Him I repeat it: not because I delight in it *absolutely*, as neither, I am sure, did He, nor does He. He would rather that the natural order were preserved; and that those, who by his Father's Providence, have been made first in worldly estate, should retain their rank in his kingdom of Grace as its great ensamples. And when any of them are noble in both respects, as a few are, his delight in them must be peculiarly complacent. But when so many, rich in wordly substance, even should they have entered into the kingdom of grace, are so slow in heart and slack in hand at that kingdom's work, it cannot but be that the Judge will with special satisfaction and felicitation appoint and welcome to the highest and nearest places at his right hand those who in humble circumstances of life, by their visitings of the poor, their instructions and prayers, their self-denying pence of charity, and their Sabbath-class instruction of the young, showed a warmth of heart in his work which He never witnessed in the others. The hour of righteous adjustment has come. Neither angel nor saint is glad to see the first made last; but great is the rejoicing to see the last made first. And those that are postponed, instead of being envious or feeling degraded, are the loudest in their acclamations at the justice of the award, and foremost to congratulate their once disesteemed brethren and sisters on their exaltation—*humbly asking their pardon*—(how much of this there will be in that day!) — saying they see now, when their judgment is disabused of all the sophistications of the pride of the world, that they were the honour and safety of the Church, and that as for themselves, they wonder at the mercy which has admitted them into the kingdom at all.

Before I close the illustration of this topic, I must address a word especially to our humble friend the widow, whose objection induced it.* That Sabbath

---

* This fancy picture, together with two that follow, though suitable enough for popular discourse, I would withdraw, as somewhat incongruous amid these polemics. But I fear some who heard the tales preached

you will remember, when in an emergency of the Missionary cause a special contribution was requested, our exemplary christian sister, Mrs. B———, out of her abundance, put into the plate a promissory Bank note of Twenty Pounds. We who witnessed it, being persuaded it was a *sincere* contribution, calculated that it might be entered to her credit in the Heavenly Register as a large ingot of gold. You followed, having heard a whisper of her munificence—admiring her, thanking the Lord for her; but with a sad heart in remembrance of former days of plenty, with your face averted that neither the collector might recognise you, nor you yourself see the pittance, furtively-like, approached, and slipped in a penny—it was all your living—there was not another left at home for tomorrow's breakfast—and hurried past. Listen now, when I tell you what occurred, and be ashamed of your faithless objections. He who once sat visibly over against the Treasury noting the contributions, and equally sits now, though invisibly, over against the collection-plate, lifted up his voice to the registering angel: The widow Mary—a diamond of purest water—value, two ingots of virgin gold.

2d,—The mistake made by many, in calculating the amount of the reward by the *bulk* of the work, is small compared with that made in calculating by the *nature* of the work. How is it, that notwithstanding

would complain. I am sure a certain Theophilus would. The *theologians* must therefore excuse me.

all the preaching and writing and talking about the spirituality of Christian worship and service, the idea of good working should be connected principally, if not entirely, with such acts and exercises as these—the observing of Sabbath ordinances, contributing for the relief of the poor, keeping Sabbath classes, and contributing to the funds of the Church, the school, the Infirmary, and Missionary Society? All these and similar works are excellent, and if well performed will be well rewarded. But there is other work which in its nature is more excellent, and will be rewarded with higher dignity in the kingdom—work purely *mental*— labour of the soul. A mere sketch of this interesting topic would occupy a large space. Besides, part of it will present itself again under another department of the subject. I will therefore satisfy myself with presenting two illustrative cases as specimens.

The first is that of the youth Theophilus, warmly companionative, emulous, fond of admiration and praise. He is solicited to unite in a projected night's diversion of the *establishment*. The temptation is great—he is the best singer of songs, the best teller of humorous stories, and, as having been well practised, when a boy, the best dancer of them all. The opportunity would be most favourable for display, and gaining applause; and as being far from home he could take the liberty of the unseasonable hours, without fear of rebuke. But he has been told of the unseemly excesses of a former *re-union;* and in the fear of his father's God, and the love of his mother's Saviour, he resolves he will not expose himself to the danger; and he stedfastly resists all importunities, flatteries and mockeries—not because he has no relish for mirth, on the contrary that is keen —not because he despises either the flatteries or the mockeries; on the contrary he is very sensitive to them, and it is with much pain of heart that he retires to his lodgings, and shuts himself up in solitude for the night, for the commandment of God is upon him. Well, when all the rest of them are so lively in their merry-making, degenerating by the witching hour into the immodest dance, the corrupt jest, the profane and licentious song, with sip after sip of the poison-bowl exciting more bad thoughts, more bad words, more bad *gestures*, as the Westminster Moralists distinguish, and more bad actions; and when the observant God turns away from the offensive sight of the revellers to look upon his faithful child sleeping soundly in the darkness, He regards him as working out the great work of a valorous self-denial. So the instruction to the recording angel is: Theophilus *sleeps well;* mark him high for reward.

As an instance of another great work of this class, observe now the case of his sister at home. When she lies exhausted after a paroxysm of her consumptive cough, and friends express their sympathy, she opens her weary eyes, and looking upwards smilingly, says, "Though He slay me, yet will I trust in Him; He gave his hands and his feet to be nailed to the cross for me, and He is now taking me home to Himself." What is your Sabbath-class keeping?—Nay, my young friends

OBEDIENCE.

—it is not fair to bring you into the comparison—What was her own Sabbath-class keeping, and her Dorcas work, and her visiting of the poor down the Vennel compared with this "perfecting of the work of patience?" And is there no reward in store for it, when yet it is the most difficult of all work, and not surpassed by any other in the glorifying of God? So the instruction for record is: Eusebia *dies well;* mark her high.

I'll tell you what—you who are poor, hungered, and ill-clad and cold, despised, racked with pain, distempered in nerves, ill-mated in marriage, vexed with bad children, bereft of good children, widowed, the victims of broken vows, ruined in character by false accusations, bankrupt-smitten—you, and all such, let me tell you, you have a great advantage above many; you have an opportunity by working at the work of Patience to gain for yourselves crowns of peculiar lustre. And let my felicitation be received, without suspecting that it is tendered in a spirit of compassionate flattery, when I express myself with discrimination, and do not say, of the very brightest lustre. Patience and Charity! Who shall invidiously compare them in order to make a preference? In that day the Judge addressing them will say, Patience and Charity, my much loved daughters! you have both acted your parts well in yonder old world of misery, which had equal need of both of you. Equal crowns and thrones are provided for you. Welcome equally into your Father's Joy! So arm in arm and *pari passu* they enter in.

I have thus endeavoured to account for what I persist in characterising as a phenomenon, that when the Word of God abounds in promises, that He will acknowledge the well doing of his faithful children with large and distinctive rewards, there should yet be so few who are animated in the discharge of their duty by the prospect. Some will be ready to say that surely error lurks somewhere in my exposure, since it is almost impossible to imagine that the whole of the church, especially in this day of intelligence, should, with a small exception, be in a state of error on a subject of such importance. Well, though it may be difficult for some to conceive of this it is very easy for me, when I read in the history of the past of the like having often occurred before; yea, when I see the like, in many other respects, exhibiting itself at the present day—intelligent and pious men and women, through formalism, educational prepossessions, slavish reverence of pastoral priesthood and favourite authors, sectarian zeal of party, personal conceit that they are already *finished* in their religious education, and many other evil principles besides, inimical to the cause of truth—remaining insensible to many of the plainest dictates of scripture, reason, and common sense; yea, entertaining notions and fancies denounced and contradicted by the threefold authorization. On the present occasion, however, I do not propound any novelty. It is a case of deterioration of which I complain; and I plead for the revival of a prominent doctrine of all the churches of the Reformation, and of all their eminent theologians for more than a century afterwards: I plead for that to which the Westminster Divines have given an unequivocal testimony in their Confession, and to which eminent preachers and writers have occasionally borne witness, all along in our history, down to the present day of a pretentious spurious evangelicalism, and of a cowardly fear of being reported "not sound" by presumptuous popular ignorance; so that the proclamation of the cheering promise of the Gospel, that all Christian good works shall be munificently rewarded, has nearly been extinguished throughout the land. Of the first fact, that the doctrine was a favourite one with the Churches of the Reformation there is no doubt; and there is as little of the second, that it is now nearly extinct in our so-called evangelical preaching. The only point in the subject about which there is any doubt is the state of sentiment among *the people*.

That it is greatly deficient is unquestionable. But I am anxious, for the credit of the Church, that the weight of the complaint and accusation be reduced as much as possible; and in looking round for alleviations, I perceive one in a state of mind which I am persuaded many will recognise as being very much their own experience. When at first they addressed themselves to their work of piety and benevolence, the calculation that they should be rewarded for it did not perhaps form an element of that combination of motives by which they were influenced to enter upon it. But now that they are in the midst of it, when they reflect on the anxiety, the toil, the expenditure, the self-denial, possibly opprobrium and mockery to which they are subjected in the prosecution of what they regard duty; and especially when their neighbours, some of them fellow church members, sit at home at their ease, reading entertaining books, and feasting, and amusing themselves with their friends, and active only in making themselves wealthy and respectable in the world—doing nothing, suffering nothing, for either religion or humanity, and parting with so little, and that grudgingly, to save character and be rid of the importunity of that most abhorred of nuisances, the collector with his subscription book;—when our zealous self-denying brethren reflect on all this, it is at once an intellectual and a moral impossibility that the thought do not arise in their minds that "the righteous Lord, who loveth righteousness, and whose countenance doth behold the upright," will, on the day of the "manifestation" of his children, signalise their faithfulness with *distinction* in his kingdom.—But there supervenes the reflection that this may be that impure self-righteousness which preachers denounce so vehemently, with "filthy rags" for their theme. So they endeavour to expel the thought as being an insinuation of the Tempter; but it will not be expelled. As introduced by correct views of God's character and government —by the special promises of his Word, recurring so constantly in their reading of it—and by the influence of the Advocate, the Comforter, together with the strong recommendation of common sense, it keeps possession of the heart, secretly and quietly pervading it, with happy expectations of compensation. Its emotions and calculations are indeed much repressed and restrained by the adverse declamations of a heretical orthodoxy; and altogether, both at entering on the work and in the course of its execution, it is unworthy of the high promise of God, given for the animation and encouragement of his children in their well-doing.—But though this testimony is weak, in the circumstances it is valuable, as saving the Church, as the family of God, from the charge of being universally and totally insensible to the assurance of the heavenly Father, that "He is not unrighteous to forget their work and labour of love," but will reward their bountiful sowing with a bountiful reaping, as distinguished from the spare reaping of those who sow sparingly.

In turning these illustrations to a more direct practical account, I call on you, Christian brethren, to realize clearly your standing as members of the Redeemed Family of God. All depends on that being your state; and the stronger your persuasion of it is, ascending into assurance, the better will it be for every good end, but especially that about which I am at present more particularly concerned—the gaining of a great quantity of Good Works out of you, when you work with the feeling and consciousness of working under the observation of a Father's eye. There is a gratifying measure of good working among us; but I am jealous of you, brethren. I fear that it is to a great extent the conscientious work of good *servants* to a master, who has given them *refuge*, and whom they feel themselves under obligations to serve in gratitude for the refuge, without being animated by that spirit of Adoption which calculates, that an observant Father will reward his children for their dutifulness at *home*. Let this great evil be remedied. Take means for strengthening your persuasion of being of the adopted number. Meditate on the position of a believer in Christ being a child of God; and then let it be with a free heart, disabused of all the sophistications of a spurious orthodoxy, that you lay hold on the children's promise, and animate yourselves with it —" always abounding in the work of the Lord, forasmuch as ye know that your labour is not in vain in the Lord." (1 Cor. xv. 58). And if on revealing the state of your mind to your friends, they should call you *mercenary*, as being actuated in your labours and charities, partly at least, by the expectation of a recompense, answer them, that whatever they may mean by the opprobrious imputation they implicate Christ in the censure; for He, "*for the joy that was set before Him*, endured the Cross, despising the shame, and is set down at the right hand of the throne of God." (Heb. xii. 2.) The prospect of being rewarded with that exaltation, contributed greatly to his patient endurance of the Cross; and we are specially directed to "Look to Him" as our Exemplar in this respect.* You can easily bear, brethren, being called mercenary, when it is in Looking unto Jesus you have acquired the spirit.

* This Example of Christ is afterwards illustrated under Resignation.

Although, on account of the prevailing ignorance and insufficient or perverse teaching on the subject, the illustrations of this topic have been greatly prolonged, yet for the same reasons it is necessary that they be prolonged a little further, in answer to this charge of Mercenariness.

A school of ethical Philosophers maintains that *virtue* is entirely *disinterested*—that its well-doing is actuated simply by a sense of duty or a love of what is right; and that when a calculation of self-profit enters into the motivity, it corrupts it, and reduces the moral value of the action. Correspondently, a school of Divines maintains that genuine *piety* is entirely disinterested—that it loves God simply on account of his essential or personal excellence, with the love of what is called the Love of Moral Approbation or esteem; and that its obedience to his law, though rendered primarily under a sense of creature obligation, is influenced to a great extent by *sympathy* with One so good, so as to gratify Him with what it knows by his law will please Him—without being in the least degree actuated by the selfish consideration of any advantage redounding to the devout worshipper. This *pietism*, as it has been called, has been advocated by names in high repute; and I doubt not but that some to whom it is for the first time presented, will regard it with favour; but a few remarks will be sufficient to shew that it is not even a devout imagination.

Observe what is precisely the state of the question. All agree that the prime motive of all virtuous and pious action is a sense of duty, connected with an appreciation in a greater or less degree of the moral excellence of the prescribed duty, and of the moral excellence of Him who prescribes it. The only question is, if it be permissible, as a *secondary* motive, to indulge the expectation of self-profit, so as to be more animated in the work. I answer, undoubtedly, if the Master Himself hold out the prospect. Even although He had not made any promise, instead of its being presumptuous that the servant should work with greater alacrity and diligence in the hope that he might possibly be rewarded, it would show that he was well disposed towards his Master, and held him in favourable estimation for his benignity. But in the present case the promise is express.

First, in answer to the ethical *philosophers*, I contend that constitutionally the Creator has strictly connected the expectation of self-advantage with a discharge of duty. The entrance of moral evil into the world has so disturbed the original arrangement that the virtuous man must frequently work without any hope of immediate reward; but even amid the disorder, and irrespectively of any hopes for eternity, the normal course of sentiment is that dutifulness is profitable; and were it possible—though I question if it is—for a man to work himself down into a state of insensibility to the expectation, it would be a denaturalising of his Heaven-framed constitution.* *Secondly*, in

---

* I had expressed myself thus before seeing Maccovius (*see Appendix*), or having my attention called to these sentences of Butler on our natural

answer to the *theological* party professing belief in the sacred Scriptures, I contend that from beginning to end these Scriptures are replete not only with divine assurances of reward for the encouragement of the faithful, but well-recommended examples of saints, who were animated in their well-doing by the promise of their own profiting. The *pietists* admit that this was the case with the Law, and those under the Law, but deny that it obtains under the Gospel. Though the denial were consistent with the fact, the admission would be fatal to their notion, since it admits that God *once* legislated that which according to their views is an immoral principle. How profane this is! But it is not true that the principle has been excluded from the Gospel. The promise of the Reward of Grace appeals as directly to the sentiment of self-love as that of the Reward of Merit does, and the promise of the former is as characteristic of the Gospel as that of the latter is characteristic of the Law. Yea, Calvin, after having illustrated how temporal afflictions, in the character of judicial *punishments*, under the Law, are continued under the Gospel in the character of paternal *chastisements*, proceeds to illustrate with much beauty and great cogency of argument how the promises of

moral constitution :—"A due concern about our own interest or happiness, and a reasonable endeavour to secure and promote it, is *virtue*, and the contrary behaviour faulty and blameable ; since, in the calmest way of reflection, we approve [by the moral sense] of the first, and condemn the other conduct . . . By the way, this observation may help to determine what justness there is in that objection against religion, that it teaches us to be interested and selfish."—*Dissertation on the Nature of Virtue.*

the Reward of Merit made under the Law are *transferred* to the Gospel, where they stand as promises of the Reward of Grace. *(See Appendix.)* Can that, then, be a vitiating and corrupting of a man's piety with mercenariness, when he opens his heart to the inspiration of the divine promise of a reward for animating him in his duty? It has the appearance of profanity to make the appeal; and is excusable only when made for the exposure of a very profane and pernicious error. See whither it leads. In piety there are two elements—the *loving* of God, and the *obeying* of Him. Well, if it be a vitiation of *the obeying* to be actuated by the expectation of what He *will do* for us, it must be a vitiation of *the loving* to be influenced by considerations of what He *has done* for us. There cannot be a logical sequence stricter: a regard to self-interest enters as much into the latter case as the former. Accordingly, the logical Jonathan Edwards, a doctor in the *pietistic* school, maintains that these words of the apostle of love—"We love Him because He first loved us"—(1 John iv. 19)—do not by any means signify that the saints are in any respect, principally or subordinately, influenced to love God by meditations on his having loved *them*—that would be mercenary; but only this, that God's elective grace has communicated to their hearts the disinterested love of Himself, for his essential divine excellences, without which communication they would have remained insensible to these excellences! Although there has been, and is, in the Church much of it, I know not of a

OBEDIENCE. 87

more lamentable instance of the manner in which an erroneous principle will, through the force of system, induce perversion in the interpretation of the sacred oracles, even with powerful and devout minds. In the present case it erases Gratitude from the catalogue of Christian virtues, and makes a sin of singing the Twenty-Third Psalm, the most endeared song with which the Church in all ages has made its sacrifice of praise. The entire Bible—Old Testament and New— the Law and the Gospel—Reason—and the experience of all the saints unite in their testimony that the loving of God commences with the *love of gratitude*— loving Him for His conferring of benefits on self; and that from being placed in this favourable position, for contemplating the excellences of a Benefactor, the love ascends into that of *moral esteem*—loving Him for what He is in Himself—but never—no, never—without a mingling of the reflection, that in all this excellence the contemplating soul has a personal interest; so that, "O God, thou art *my* God," is the method of his song of praise and suppliant prayer.*

Hitherto I have occupied the low ground of maintaining that it is *permissible* to be actuated in our duty by the calculation of its being profitable for our own interests. But I advance, and contend that it is highly sinful to be *impassive* to the encouragement, inasmuch as it is a disregard and slighting of the promise of

* The two sentiments are illustrated at length in the author's first series of Discourses on Loving God.

God—indicates a proud presumption of being adequate to the work independently of it and from being inspired with higher motives—and derogates from the glory of God whose prerogative it is to be *disinterested* in all his ways. The notion of creature-disinterested virtue and piety invades this divine prerogative.—I advance still further. The Christian's expectation that God will reward his good works, not only does not diminish the excellence of his morality, but enhances it. There are two things requisite for making a hope a good one—the first, that it have a satisfactory *ground;* the second, that its *object* be worthy. In the Christian's case the *ground* is the promise of God, which, beside its being prudent for its sureness, it is morally commendable for him to take, as indicating his faith in God; and as for the *object*, let the conduct of his Exemplar-Lord explain it. He "for the Joy that was set before Him" in his Father's promise "endured the Cross, despising the shame." (Heb. xii. 2.) And what was that Joy which was the *object* of his hope? It was "sitting down at the right hand of the throne of God," in all the royalty of its position. Mark the *position*, in respect of its nearness to God and communion with Him; and mark the nature of the *royalty*, as to be exercised in promoting the divine glory. Such was the *object* of that hope by which the Master was inspired and sustained as the promised reward of his work; and the same is the *object* of the hope of the disciple, as a joint heir with Christ" (Rom. viii. 17), to "sit with Him in His throne"

(Rev. iii. 21, 2 Tim. ii. 12)—in all respects a sharer of his " Joy."

Mark therefore now the saint's *position* with which he expects to be rewarded—closeness to Christ, and therefore nearness to God, the intervention only assisting the communion with the Eternal Father; and mark the nature of the *royalty*, at which by his well-doing he aspires,—reigning for the promotion of the Divine glory in fellowship with Christ; and so much the better that it is *under* Him as the Superior Administrator. Is this what the Christian hopes for as a Reward? And when aiming at a large measure of it — ten cities, instead of five—he may be stimulated to abound more in charity to the widow and orphan, than is the common run of a respectable benevolence, who shall accuse him of mercenariness, but those who are inferior to him in grace, or entirely destitute of it? It needs a holy heart to be self-interested in this manner. There are many swollen with the lust of greatness and power, who would rather be bound hands and feet in shackles and fetters of iron, and cast into a dungeon, than condemned to the wearing of a crown in the kingdom of God by the side of Jesus Christ.

In concluding the argument with you, Christian brethren, I admonish you, that independently of its being sinful, you cannot, as prudent men, afford to dispense with the aid of any motive, but especially one so great as the expectation of a reward with which God addresses you, for securing the faithful and patient prosecution of your duty. Neither are you through other motives so strong, nor are your temptations to ease and wandering so few and weak, that the prospect of a reward is superfluous. And when some may say that it would be preposterous for them to expect a reward for the little they do, may not the want of proceeding in the expectation of a reward be partly, at least, the occasion of the littleness? There can be no doubt of it in the cases of many. Therefore, by an upward look of Loyalty to the Throne; by a retrospective look of Gratitude to the Cross; and not less by a prospective look to the Reward of the Crown of Righteousness, let us *constrain* our hearts to zeal in works of holiness and love.

I may not yet dismiss this topic. I have been addressing with words of encouragement the well-doers among us, not neglecting the patient in tribulation who will afterwards receive a large share of attention. But is there not another party in our company? Ah! you who, not to speak of habits and courses of well-doing, have not one act in your memories of piety and benevolence, which was not coerced by some worldly consideration, or at best by some constitutional impulse —without the recollection of one thing done, or one good emotion felt towards God and his Son Jesus Christ, with which it is possible to connect the idea of rewardableness, even when the widest comprehension is given to the terms of the Reward of Grace. How I pity you for the waste and barrenness in the *retrospect* of Life, making the *prospect* still more waste and barren! Oh! men and women too, young men and maidens, haste you out of this wilderness into which the Prince of this world has seduced you, and cross over into that territory where the children of God dwell and work, under the shining of the Sun of Righteousness, with such happy visions above and behind, and before, and all around them—with even the grave illuminated.

Resignation.

Resignation, under afflictive dispensations of Providence, is the third property of that Honouring of God as a Father, which I proposed to illustrate and enforce. Strictly considered it is a form of filial Obedience; but of such importance is it that it is entitled to a special illustration. Some have assigned it next to Faith the highest place in their valuation of Christian graces. But such preferences are, to say the least of them, indiscreet. By a picture of the meek and unmurmuring patience, which for weary years the sufferer from spinal disease has exercised and manifested, you may magnify her grace above the charity of her who has laboured and spent in the visitation of the poor; but it might be matched by the picture of the youth who, to principle, and the fear of God, has sacrificed love and prospects of wealth, and worldly elevation and honour; and overmatched by a picture of him, who, in zeal for God and the Gospel, has left behind the loves, the ease, the happy prospects of home, and voluntarily made his way into the wilds of heathenism, with the possibility before him of encountering a martyr's death. But I am in danger of committing the indiscretion which I profess to reprove. The solution of the matter is, that the faith which produced the patience in tribulation, might, in a state of health, have produced the zeal of the missionary martyr; and that that which produced the zeal of the martyr, might, if subjected to tribulation, have produced the patience of the diseased sufferer.

Proceeding to analyze this grace, I observe primarily, that the patience under affliction, which is entitled to the name of Resignation, implies that the affliction be regarded as proceeding from the will and ordering of God. "It is the Lord," (1 Samuel iii. 18,) is the fundamental maxim. I do not refer at present so much to the manner in which this persuasion *promotes* patience, as to its being necessary to give it the character of a devout feeling. For anything I know there may be a patience, the expression of which is, "There is no use of complaining; the evil has befallen me according to the laws of nature and was my inevitable fate;" but if such a patience there be, and not a mere pretence of it, or a dull and rude insensibility, it is evidently not a religious affection. The resigned Christian is, on the other hand, convinced that God is the author of all his afflictions, either by direct commission or permission, or restraining or withholding what would have prevented them.

As just stated, I give this conviction of a special overruling Providence the first place in the illustration, as being necessary to the religious character of the patience; but though it will somewhat anticipate future illustrations, there is a particular mode in which it promotes and facilitates the exercise of the grace which it is convenient to notice here.—In want of this conviction, or if it be but slight, how ready are parents, for instance, when they have been bereaved of their children, to engage their minds with regrets that certain things were done and others not done, both by themselves and physicians—as if by a different treatment their children would have been saved. Not only do such *reflections* embitter the bereavement, but they occupy the mind either so as to exclude the proper consolation, or by mingling with it, greatly to reduce its strength. It may be quite true that there were such neglects and mistakes in the treatment; but let the thoughts of them be dismissed by the reflection, It is the Lord—that He having his purpose to serve, permitted the mismanagement; and then let the soul deal with Him alone, as the Author of the death. That might indeed only exacerbate the affliction for an ungodly man, and cause him to " charge God foolishly " and blaspheme. But I speak at present of the resignation of God's children. Let it be disencumbered of these vain regrets and *reflections*. Ah! what sorry work they make of the heart, with their distractions, in its attempts to find consolation in God! The advantage, or rather necessity of thus excluding from the meditations, thoughts of the proximate cause of the affliction appears especially in cases in which the *wickedness* of man has been employed as the instrument. The conviction and reflection that God's hand has directed the instrument may not indeed entirely prevent or assuage your anger—for God did not make the man wicked, but only found him in his wickedness a fit agent for His designed affliction of you; so that you have a social right to be angry with the evil doer: but the conviction that God is the original Author of your calamity will save the heart from much of that burning indignation with which it would be affected, if it saw nothing but the malice of man to be the cause of its grief; and will give it more freedom for a submissive contemplation of the ordination of God—as if it had been the lightning, or the storm, or the flood, or the pestilence, or the wild beast, which he hath let loose upon you, or commissioned, or directed. "So let him curse," said David, submissively, of the execrations of Shimei, "because the Lord hath said unto him, Curse David: who shall then say, Wherefore hast *thou* done so? (2 Sam. xvi. 10.)* This was an extreme in David's state of depression of spirits. The malicious rebel deserved a punishment, though it might not be to be transfixed with Abishai's spear; but the mitigation of his wrath proceeded from a sound principle, which it would have been better, at least for his memory in this world, to have preserved till the end, instead of giving on his death-bed that atrocious counsel which served

---

* It may be questioned whether the "thou" refer to God or to Shimei. It does not much affect the case whichever of the views be adopted.

his son with an apology for one of the most dastardly acts of cruelty which the annals of despotism have recorded. (1 Kings ii. 9 and 44). How blessed the contrast of *our* two Kings !—Father and Son, too—" God commendeth his love towards us, in that while we were yet sinners, Christ (as commissioned by Him) died for us."—"Then said Jesus (as they crucified Him) Father, forgive them, for they know not what they do." (Romans v. 8; Luke xxiii. 34.) Greater than both Solomon and David are here.—This reflection, by the way: I proceed with the illustration of our topic.

The heart being well established in the maxim, " It is the Lord," the next persuasion of that resignation by which the saints honour him as a Father, is that the afflictions of His providence are mercifully designed for their advantage; and that though they see not the reasons now, they shall see them hereafter, and be fully satisfied that the treatment was the best which they could have received. From this it will be seen that resignation is not merely of a negative character—an unmurmuring, unrepining submission under affliction to the divine will—but positively, acquiescence in it—reconcilement of the mind to it—a measure of contentment, satisfaction, or pleasedness, not with the affliction but that you are afflicted. A child may nauseate the drug, and cry when the cup is put into his hand, but it is his Father who is the Physician, neither the wisdom nor kindness of whose prescription he can doubt; so it is with a measure of thankfulness for the care taken of him that He empties the cup of its bitter draught

Mourning, but not *murmuring*, is an old distinction deservedly in great repute, and it would be much if all the children of sorrow had attained to the condition; yet it does not adequately express the grace of Resignation. It wants a notice of the hope of reparation or of the persuasion of advantage which counterbalances the mourning—counterbalances it, I say, but does not dispel it, and only mitigates it by dividing with it the mind's occupations. For there is as much need of a defence of the lawfulness of *mourning*, as of shewing the insufficiency of *not murmuring;* both for the sake of the sufferers themselves, who are ready to suspect that their *mourning* indicates a want of resignation; and for the rebuke of ignorant neighbours who may censure them for their lamentations. A man may be thoroughly persuaded that the cutting off of his right arm is the best thing that can be done for him—as being necessary to save his life; but would that persuasion save him from the pain of the amputation? Yea, would it prevent him from going about mourning all his days the loss of his arm?—There is more than this: though he were persuaded that his arm would in a few years be restored to him in a state of greater vigour than ever, would this prevent his mourning its present loss? The persuasion would suppress *murmuring*, as he reflected, otherwise I would have died; and it would mitigate the *mourning* by its counterbalancing reflections of advantage; but it would not render either body or mind insensible to *pain* and *privation*, to endure which, without mournful expression in tears and sighs and moanings would be as little "good *grace*" as "commendable *nature;*" it would be the savage pride and defiance of the Indian.

From the complexity of the nature of Resignation, it is impossible, in any circumstances to *define* it otherwise than vaguely: say, Acquiescent submission under affliction to the will of God. But besides this, it is impracticable, at the present stage of our illustration, even to *describe* it by circumlocutory phrases, before we have examined what are the special considerations of the Divine purpose, by which the acquiescence is produced. In this examination I shall presently engage; but previously remark here, as being the most convenient time for the observation, that the elements of the *counterbalancing* Hope should be as much as possible *mingled* with the elements of mourning. When the mind dwells on recounting the various evils of the affliction, designing to turn to a consideration of the grounds of consolation after it has completed the review of miseries,—by the brooding it is often so overwhelmed or excited into agony, as to be incapacitated for the consolatory contemplation. Beware of *brooding*. As element after element of the sorrow presents itself, interject an element of comfort. In this way not only will the paroxysm of grief be moderated, but sometimes entirely allayed, from the mind being transported into wide regions of Hopefulness. *Haud ignarus,* &c.

Having, in a general way, described what Resignation

is, I proceed to a more particular analysis of the Grace under an answer to the question, What are the special considerations and reflections by which it is produced and cherished? This will serve to make our views less vague and more definite.

I answer, *First*, Negatively, that mere considerations of God's Sovereign right to afflict us, in any way as it may please Him, since as his creatures we are but as clay in the hands of the potter, will not produce resignation. Such reflections are not calculated even to repress murmurings. The sufferer will complain that he was created a sentient being to be so anguished and tormented, undeservedly, or without respect to his own future advantage. How much less are they calculated to produce that acquiescence which is characteristic of resignation? It is astonishing that so many of our divines should inculcate resignation on this ground, violating all common sense. I cannot answer them in the question of the Creator's physical right to afflict, in mere arbitrary sovereignty; but I can answer in the question of the creature's responsibility. He is not responsible for being contentedly acquiescent in being subjected to suffering without being a criminal, or without being assured of compensation. And remember that it is a child's state of mind, in regard of his Father's treatment, which is at present the subject of consideration. Would that be the honouring of a Father which was a mere doglike submission under the whip on the much misinterpreted "potter and clay" principle?* Even though the sufferer were persuaded that the Divine Sovereign was employing his sufferings for a good end, in the administration of the government of the universe, he would not, he could not be *resigned*, so long as he had no reason for believing that any advantage would redound to himself. It is dishonouring to God to represent Him as either requiring, or as claiming a right to require, that any of his creatures whom He has constituted rational and with moral calculation, should submit acquiescently to suffering on such irrational and unscriptural principles.

In connection with the above, or rather as a particular manifestation of the same error, I notice that it is not Resignation when a man may merely argue with himself that there is *no use* in complaining under afflictions appointed by God, since it is impossible to resist his power. I know not if there be any one who endeavours to still the commotions of his heart by pleading with it in this manner. But I know that there are many who advise their friends to try it: who on making their calls of courtesy on the afflicted, will remonstrate with them that really they should not *take it on* so heavily and cry so much, since none of us can resist Providence, and must just submit to its ways. The poor creatures know of

* Jeremiah xviii. 6. The clay on which the potter wrought with the design of making a vessel of excellence was marred under his hand; so he made it one of inferior worth. Such was the imagery of the parable. And what, according to the context, is the moral application? Nothing can be plainer or more opposed to the vulgar interpretation. It is, that Israel, designed of the Lord to be a vessel of honour, was marred by sin, so that in indignation He turned its clay into one of dishonour. This was not an act of arbitrary Sovereignty but of righteous judgment.

nothing better to say. It is the old heathenism, that we must just submit to our Fate. Oh, that they would stay at home! those courtesy sympathisers, or satisfy themselves with leaving their cards or names at the door of the house of mourning; till they have learned from the Gospel to be comforters instead of wearisome tormentors of those for whom they affect sympathy.

Secondly,—Still negatively, in answer to the present question, I observe that the reflection that you *deserve* the affliction for your sins, will not contribute much, if anything, to make you resigned. I do not dispute that the term *deserved* may be used properly enough of some of the afflictions of God's children. But in any case it is advisable to avoid it. It is ready to convey the idea of *punishment*, which we have already seen, and will yet see more clearly, is never the character of the afflictions of God's family. And I counsel you, brethren, never to use it in reference either to your own afflictions or to those of your Christian friends. I will furnish you with the proper expression afterwards; meantime I observe, that if you regard your afflictions only as being *deserved*, it may suppress murmurings, and make you submissive and humble, but will fail of making you resigned. The penitent criminal, when led forth to execution, may, without murmuring, confess that his punishment is just: but it would be a misuse of language to say he is resigned.

Having answered the question negatively, I proceed to state affirmatively, and explain, what are the considerations and reflections which produce and cherish this eminent grace. We have seen generally that there must be a persuasion on the part of the sufferer, that a benevolent regard to his own advantages have partly, at least, influenced the commission of the affliction. But there is great variety in the designs of the Lord; and, according to the variety, is the manifestation of his love; and according to that again, is there a difference in the complexion of the Resignation.

So far as I can divine, there are principally four ends which God has in view by afflicting his children. Perhaps seldom, if ever, is there any case in which He designs to secure only one of these. And though it is a legitimate exercise reflectively to inquire what may be his particular or principal intentions, saying with Job, "Shew me wherefore Thou contendest with me," (x. 2,) yet we should be cautious in determining peremptorily what they are; lest by mistake we omit the great object, and lose much of the designed advantage. We should imagine all kinds of good reasons, and learn something from its being possible that each may have a part in the divine intention.—The need for this caution will appear in the course of the illustration.

FIRST, There are afflictions *Corrective:*—Fatherly Chastisements; designed of God for the reform of his children when they err; or for rousing them into activity when they have fallen into a state of languor or indolence. If you are in the course of acquiring or indulging any evil habit—or are allowing the world to engross your mind, to the neglect of all things spiritual and heavenly—or are in a state of prayerless declension, nearing to apostacy—and if all the remonstrances and strivings of God's Spirit within your conscience have been resisted and quenched,—I appeal to what remains of moral sensibility in your heart, if He would not be wanting in fatherly care of you, did He not take down the Rod of his Providence and smite your obduracy into submission—afflicting you in whatever way He sees best adapted for humbling you, and bringing you to your senses, as when it is said of the prodigal, "he came to himself." I press the appeal: Would He be a good father if He acted otherwise? Does not he who spares the Rod hate his child? And when by its smart it may have awakened you out of your dangerous sleep, what can you do but "kiss" it, and thank Him who "hath appointed" it? He has mercifully sent you what you *needed:* that is the word for you, instead of *deserved.* Use it thoughtfully: It contains a principal secret of Resignation.

Observe carefully, brethren, that God's paternal chastisements are ranked in the Scripture among the best indications of his love: for the obvious reasons, that an affectionate parent feels the afflicting of his child to be a painful exercise for himself; and that a careless parent will not submit to the trouble. Listen to the "exhortation which speaketh unto you as unto children," and which it is strange (remarks Lady Powerscourt) we should be so ready to "forget," like the Hebrew Christians of old, when we have so much need of it: "My son, despise not thou the chastening of the Lord, nor faint when thou art rebuked of Him: for whom the Lord loveth He chasteneth, and scourgeth every son whom He receiveth. If ye endure chastening, God dealeth with you as with sons; for what son is he whom the father chasteneth not? But if ye be without chastisement, whereof all are partakers, then are ye bastards, and not sons. Furthermore, we have had fathers of our flesh which corrected us, and we gave them reverence: shall we not much rather be in subjection unto the Father of spirits and live? For they verily for a few days chastened us after their own pleasure; but He for our profit, that we might be partakers of his holiness. Now no chastening for the present seemeth to be joyous but grievous: nevertheless afterward it yieldeth the peaceable fruit of righteousness unto them which are exercised thereby." (Heb. xii. 5-11.) Should any reader have *skipped* this quotation, I beseech him to look back and read it thoughtfully, and not "forget its exhortation." Abound though the Bible does in consolation, it does not contain much that is more needful.—It will recur under the illustration of another topic. At present I appeal to it in evidence, that instead of the presence of affliction being a reason for murmuring and repining, it is the absence of it which gives the exempted some reason for suspecting that they may be reprobated as aliens, who have no part nor lot in the divine family.—So plainly does this appear, at first view, to be the proper import of the words, that some, whom all their friends hold in high estimation, are troubled with doubts of their adoption, because the lines have fallen unto them in such pleasant places, that it may be well said of them, they have no cross to bear, and that they are "without chastisement." The difficulty—for although scarcely noticed by the commentators, it is one of considerable magnitude—seems to be resolvable only on the principle that the apostle speaks of what is *normal*, or the general state of children—that they need to be chastised. Just, however, as in human families children occasionally appear, for whom there is no need of such severe discipline, is it not rather to be expected, than considered strange, that the like should occur in the divine family? I am accordingly persuaded that there are to be found saints for whose heavenly training—admonitions, warnings, reproofs and remonstrances of the Spirit are sufficient, without there being need to have recourse to the correction of the Rod. Though this opinion were wrong, it could do little harm; so few are they who are "without chastisement," and who could be deluded by it into a state of false security.

An important observation remains to be made before concluding the illustration of this topic. The consideration of the mere correction of error and reclaiming to duty would have afforded a satisfactory reason for submitting to affliction with acquiescence. But there is much more than this. A patient, confiding endurance of what your sin deserves (I take advantage of the expression for a time) becomes of itself a *rewardable grace*. The profiting is twofold: not only does the affliction recover and re-establish you; it contributes to your exaltation. It may be said with propriety that advantage has been taken of your sin to raise you, as a reward of your patience under the chastisement, to a higher position in the kingdom than that to which otherwise you might have attained. Many acknowledge that it has been good for them that they have been afflicted, in consideration of the manner in which they have thereby regained the position from which they had fallen, and been made more careful of their ways for the future (Ps. cxix. 67 and 71); but it would assist their resignation if they reflected that the exercise of patience itself, in the way to recovery, greatly advanced their spiritual interests. There is another helpful consideration, which will be noticed under another topic. But enough has been adduced at present for enforcing the apostle's concluding appeal: " Wherefore lift up the hands which hang down and the feeble knees; and make straight paths for your feet, lest that which is lame be turned out of the way; but let it rather be healed." (Heb. xii. 12, 13.)

SECOND. There are afflictions *Preventive:*—designed of God to save his children from spiritual evils, or greater temporal afflictions, which He foresees would meet them in the natural course of things, and out of the way of which He turns them aside by affliction, or hides them by it in its shade "until the calamity be overpast." It would be presumptuous judgment to say that this prevention of future evil is as frequently the design of affliction as the correction of existing evil. But there can be no doubt that in many cases it is the principal, if not the only design; and that both the resignation of the saint and the fatherly character of God sustain much loss by its being so little considered. For our own consolation and His honour we should calculate that although we did not see any danger in the distance, He did, and mercifully withdrew us from the sphere of its operation.

According to the distinction in the statement just made for illustration, the prevention may be only that of some greater temporal affliction; as when what is called an accident, by which the sufferer lost a limb, prevented him from sailing according to his purpose in a ship which was wrecked. Life-long though his lameness and the impairing of his activity be, the reflection that it prevented his death will, or should, suppress all rising murmurings, and make him resigned under his loss. Again, how many can tell that those divinely permitted broken vows of love, by which their hearts were at the time so anguished and desolated, saved them, as now appears, from lives of misery, so as to make them thankful for the escape! They should have considered at the time, that this or something similar might be the design of their divine Guardian; so that the bitterness of their affliction would have been mitigated.

Illustrations such as the above might be multiplied to a great extent, and any one can supply them for himself. I therefore turn to illustrate the other part of the statement—that afflictions are often designed for the prevention of *spiritual evils.*

Take the two following examples: the first that of a youth prostrated on his bed for years by spinal disease. When his acquaintance visit him, and he sees how their minds are improving under the culture of their privileges, and hears of the well-doing in which they are actively engaged; and especially when he does not feel that his own heart is the subject of any special process of spiritualization, how ready he is to murmur, if he ask that question only,—Wherein has my affliction profited me? But whenever he turns the reflection the other way, and begins to imagine what dangers may have been lurking in his path, away from and out of the road of which the Lord has laid him down on that bed as an asylum of safety, what a bed of thanksgiving it becomes to him! And when his mind is thus directed it will not continue merely an exercise of *imagining* dangers, which God may have foreseen, though he himself saw them not. There are few who, in such circumstances, will not detect and discover that there was something in their constitutional temperament, or their education, or connections, or employment, which had a seducing or an ensnaring tendency. What, then, does it signify though the *positive profiting* of that sickness does not appear? Be thankful that it has saved your soul from ruin.—The other example is that of one who complains that the desolation of his business has not only not wrought for him any spiritual good, but actually deteriorated his mind through the bitterness of anxiety, and almost "choked the word" within him. I ask again, what does that signify in comparison of the greater, the complete loss of all divine and spiritual principle which, the Lord foresaw, wealth and worldly pleasures and honours would have occasioned him? When a less evil saves from a greater does not the less become a subject of grateful thanksgiving?

The preventive mercy of DEATH demands a special consideration. Of this subject, at once so full of mourning and so full of consolation, I select, as an exemplar case, that of a mother who has been bereaved of her child. There are two elements in her grief. *First*, there is a sense of her own personal loss; when besides the pain of being presently deprived of an endeared companionship, and an object on which to lavish her attention and care, which had so expanded and dilated her heart, and made such wide room for itself, but which room is now left a yearning void; when besides this, I say, all these *hopes* are cut off which she cherished of the honour and help she would enjoy in the manhood of that child, in whom she thought she perceived so many indications and promises of future excellence. As she recounts these promises, and weeps over her extinguished hopes, it is somewhat ungracious to call upon her to reflect that, notwithstanding all these favourable indications in childhood, he might, had his life been prolonged, have fallen under the temptations which the Lord saw would overtake him; and like many grown-up sons of other parents, who in childhood promised as fairly as he, have proved the heart-break, the shame and torment of her life, whereas by that death he is saved to her hopes, that she will receive him back glorified in the everlasting kingdom of heaven. I have admitted that it is somewhat ungracious and invidious to call upon her to imagine the possibility of the moral depravation of one so dear, had he lived to be tempted; yet, I contend that it is her duty to give that possibility a part in her meditations; both piously for the defence of the fatherly character of God, and prudently for the ease of her heart in reducing the pain of disappointed hopes. For anything she knows, not only would these hopes never have been fulfilled in his prolonged life, but answered with deep distress. So that the state of the account is distinctly this: She is *not sure* that in manhood he would have been a comfort to her—not sure that he would not have been a vexation to her; but through his death is *made sure* that she will never be distressed by his misconduct, as some of her friends are by the misconduct of their sons—sure, which they are not respecting theirs, that she will recover him glorified in the day of the manifestation of the children of God—his glory being certain, and the only thing uncertain being that she will prove faithful and be there to behold it. Let her be faithful then.

The *Second* element of her grief is similar to the first;—it is her *sympathy* with her deceased child, as having been removed from happy prospects which her mind busies itself in fancying. How strong soever her assurance may be that his soul is with Christ in safe and happy keeping against the day of Resurrection—even when the glory of the Intermediate state is magnified, as it often is, much beyond any scriptural authority—it will not suffice, as all experience proves, for preventing the recurrence of these regrets of his being cut off from hopes; and something more is necessary for allaying the pain than either the persuasion of his present happiness or of his future glory. It is necessary to attack the foundation of these disappointed hopes; so as if not to dissipate them entirely, at least to diminish their force by the interjection of counterbalancing ideas of lamentable possibilities. And here there is no need of having recourse to what was formerly admitted to be a somewhat ungracious way of administering consolation—the suggestion of the possibility of her child's future immorality. It is enough to refer to what is not uncommon in the course of virtuous life. Who assures you, Mother, that he would have been so happy, as you imagine, if his life had been prolonged? Possibly, the Lord saw the reverse—the development of some disease lurking in his constitution which would have consigned him for years to a bed of anguish—some fraud in a fellow-merchant which would have agonised him with all a bankrupt's wretchedness—the desolation of heart which is inflicted by the broken vow of love—failure in the competition for office or place, withering all his future life with chagrin and disappointment—some calumny which he had not the means of refuting, and burdened with which he would have descended into a dishonoured grave—something, perhaps, still more miserable, the imagination of the possibility of which befalling him should make you feel as if you were cruel to him, when you regret that the Lord has removed him out of the way of it, and taken him to Himself to secure him from all harm, against that day when all shall be satisfactorily resolved.*

It is not the death of children alone over which mourners should console themselves as a *preventive* affliction. To men advanced in life also is it frequently sent in mercy to save them from approaching calamities. And it is in reference to adults that the Scriptural phrase which is popularly appropriated to children, is originally used: "Merciful men are taken away, none considering that the righteous is *taken away from the evil to come.*" (Isaiah lvii. 1). Adverting to only one species of evil as an example—who does not know of parents that have died, of whom we may say, How mercifully the Lord dealt with them in taking them away before they saw the profligacy of their sons and the shame of their daughters! And who does not know others of whom we are ready to say that it would have been better for them had they died when their children

---

* "'Whom the gods love, die young,' was said of yore;
And many deaths do they escape by this:—
The death of friends, and that which pains still more,
The death of friendship, love, youth—all that is,
Except mere breath; and since the silent shore
Awaits at last even those whom longest miss
The old Archer's shafts, perhaps an early grave,
Which men weep over, may be meant to save."

were infants, though it had been with the sore feeling of leaving them to the mercy of the public Alms House, than that they should have lived to be so tormented by them as they are at the present day? Weep not for the Christian dead as if they had been taken away from better prospects: Weep for the living, who are left to struggle with the miseries of the wilderness.—These reflections, appropriate at all times, are specially suitable for our generation. Let no appearances nor speculations deceive you, brethren: days of tribulation, the like of which this world has never experienced, are at hand; when those who may be living shall envy the lot of those who have died. God's great controversy with the sins of the nations will proceed in its dreadful course, and when at last the storm bursts and the vial is emptied, the exclamation of the living shall be— Happy they who enjoy the shelter of the grave!

So much of our subject remains to be illustrated that I must satisfy myself with having produced these few specimens of the manner in which Resignation may be promoted by the consideration of afflictions being frequently designed to be *preventive* of greater evils. And in summing up the advantages of the case I observe, that not only is there the gain of a mind reconciled to present affliction, in the thought that it may have saved from a greater; and the gain of an improved spirituality under the discipline; but also the gain of that reward of grace with which the patience itself will be acknowledged in the day of Recompence.

THIRD.—There are afflictions *Preparative.*—All afflictions whatever of God's children are partly designed to prepare their souls for the eternal inheritance. But those which I have especially in view at present are such as are designed and employed as causes of future temporal advantage; as when the selling of Joseph into slavery by his brethren, when his father mourned over him as dead, was permitted and directed to the end of the saving and exaltation of the whole family. How many there are who are ready gratefully to bear witness that in like manner, the losses which at the time they lamented bitterly, proved efficient causes of their subsequent prosperity! So that it is the duty of the afflicted in many cases to moderate their grief by reflecting that possibly the Lord's dealings with *them* may be similarly designed. I admit, however, though this be plainly reasonable, that its influence in producing and cherishing Resignation is not very strong, and that the grand motives must be sought for in other directions. Nevertheless since it contains a measure of relief, it should not be despised. Our hearts cannot afford to dispense with one drop of consolation, and reconcilement of them to the will and ordination of God.—There is yet another way in which afflictions are mercifully designed to be *preparative*—preparative of the mind for enduring heavier afflictions which are imminent. She, for an example, a faithful disciple, who has been tenderly reared in youth by parents, and endearingly cherished in married life, who has experience of nothing but slight vexations, and to whose heart *sorrow* is a stranger—

how shall such a one endure that widowhood, which the Lord sees impending? He bereaves her of one of these bright boys, the most promising, she says, of all the three—introduces her to sorrow, habituates her mind to it, and strengthens—not hardens—strengthens it for bearing the dreadful stroke of widowhood—without which preparation she must have died, or been rendered useless for the training of her two remaining boys, of whom the Lord has need in his vineyard. This is no fancy picture. Many devout widows and mothers in Israel will bear witness to its being one of the ways of the Lord's mysterious yet most gracious administration, as the Father of his family. Nevertheless it cannot be employed, in the first instance, as an argument for Resignation. It would be barbarous to attempt to reconcile a mother to the loss of her child by suggesting that it might possibly be designed to prepare her mind for the loss of her husband! It is only after the catastrophe that the preparation for it may be reviewed with thanksgiving. In the mean time, consolation must be sought for in other reflections.

FOURTH.—There are afflictions *Probative;* designed to elevate the soul to a higher state of grace in order to a high degree of glory—without being in their design, specially at least, either corrective, preventive, or preparative, as already illustrated, or vicarious, to be illustrated afterwards.—*Disciplinary* is the generic term for expressing the whole of the acts of God's *training* of his children; and Probative, appears to be the best specific term for expressing those particular acts which now fall under consideration. As *probative*, however, is seldom used, *disciplinary* will be employed in the subsequent illustration, in the restricted sense indicated, as expressive of afflictions principally designed for elevating and refining the character, and especially as contradistinguished from those which are *corrective*.

Just as the Primitive Fathers, as they are called, even Augustine, did scant justice to that grand distinction of the Gospel, the Reward of Merit and the Reward of Grace, so they were wanting in a clear discernment of that other grand distinction, Judicial Punishment and Paternal Chastisement. Under Popery both of the distinctions were buried out of sight; and a very important part of the work of the Fathers of the Reformation was to bring them forth again to light. It is the latter of the distinctions in which we are at present particularly interested. And great was the service which our Reforming ancestors, and especially Calvin, in his Institutes, did for Truth and the Church, by restoring to the Canon of Scripture that twelfth chapter of the Epistle to the Hebrews, and much more similar throughout the Bible, which the Apostacy had obliterated, and the obliteration of which it perpetuates for its enslaved and blinded devotees.—Notwithstanding, however, the greatness and thankworthiness of the services of the Reformers, in this as in other matters, yet in consequence of their treatment of the subject of afflictions being almost limited to the overthrow of the imposture of Penance, their representations of the designs of affliction are defective and in some points erroneous.

The Popish Doctors maintain that all afflictions, whatsoever and of whomsoever, are penal, or *judicial punishments*. The Reformers admitted this to be the character of the afflictions of unbelievers; but contended that *fatherly chastisements* was the character of those of the faithful. In these views they are generally followed at the present day: but both the admission and contention are faulty through excess. The first almost entirely so; the second, to a large extent.

First.—Though I rather contend than deny that *national* afflictions of war, pestilence, famine, &c., are usually of the character of judicial punishments, yet I equally contend that in their special incidence on the individuals composing the nation, they are of the character of paternal discipline of one kind or another. This will not be disputed, except by the Papists, to be their character in the case of the saints. But I maintain that the same is their character in the case of unbelievers. And I claim liberty when visiting any one of this class, when lying on a bed of sickness, to assure him that God is not *punishing* him, but in his paternal mercy *chastising* him, for his recovery to the heavenly family. If on visiting I found him, instead of being sick, elated by success in some mercantile adventure, I would be scripturally warranted to remonstrate with him, " Despisest thou the riches of his goodness and forbearance and long-suffering; not knowing that the *goodness* of God leadeth [is designed to lead] thee to repentance?" (Rom. ii. 4.) These words were originally addressed by the apostle to an unbeliever, and one of a very scornful and obdurate class. And is not the analogy of the strictest order—is not the principle precisely the same, when I plead with him, should he be sick, bereaved, or made bankrupt, that the *affliction* by God, is designed for the same end? Nothing but the perversion of self-called evangelicalism will dispute it —such evangelicalism as questions the sincerity of God in his proclamation of the universal, individual call of the Gospel, to "every one," to repent and believe, in order to be saved.—I question, if under the Mediatorial Dispensation there be any *punishment* of sin in this world, except of *national* sin, which cannot be punished in Eternity, and which for the vindication of the Divine government is punished in this life, by the fall of empires or the diminution of their pomp. But in the case, for instance, of an individual blasphemer, dying with the words of cursing on his lips, it is safer to say that God has taken him away from the opportunity of committing more sin, so as to increase the weight of his condemnation, than to speak of that death as being an avenging judgment. Ah, no, ungodly men! you know nothing of Divine *punishment* as yet; all your present sorrows, howsoever bitter, are but *fatherly corrections and warnings;* what then shall be the *punishment,* when Justice erects its tribunal?

Second.—The error of characterising all the afflictions of the *saints* as being *corrective chastisements* is as great as the other and perhaps more prejudicial. It tends to hinder Resignation by mingling with it, without cause, a measure of bitterness; since chastisement implies a degree of divine displeasure, howsoever well persuaded the sufferer may be that it proceeds chiefly from fatherly love and carefulness.—Besides, it sets him on the search for sins in his heart and life which may have subjected him to the chastisement; and not seldom leads him to the inventing of imaginary evils.—I am far from denying that such self-searching is in many cases needful and profitable, and that the bitterness is inevitable and salutary: and I do not affirm that there is any case of affliction of any member of God's family into the design of which the correcting of some fault does not enter: but equally, on the other hand, I contend that no one has a right to affirm that such correction is universally an element of the design; much less that it is the principal element; and much less still that it forms the whole of the design.—If, according to the common teaching, all afflictions are chastisements, then will the most heavily afflicted saints be evinced to be the naughtiest and most obdurate and the most difficult to manage of the whole family. Can any one, even of the most uncharitable disposition in suspecting secret sins either of heart or life, possibly credit this? So far as my personal observation and biographical reading enable me to form a judgment, not a few of the most eminent saints have been the most heavily afflicted.

The difficulty—for it has been made a difficulty by defective teaching—has been already partly resolved by the illustrations of Preventive and Preparative afflictions, and I now resolve it further by the distinction of Disciplinary afflictions, as qualified at the commencement of the illustration of this topic—the afflictions of favourite saints—favourite because so faithful—designed to advance their graces to a higher degree of spiritual refinement, the Lord having in view the elevating of them to peculiar honours in his heavenly kingdom: so that the corrective element of chastisement, if it have a place at all in the design, has but a subordinate one. True, it is but few to whom this great consolation appertains; but in proportion to their fewness is the greatness of their worth, and of their claims that their rights be respected. I therefore proceed to argue the case.

First, it is reasonable that in the training of the divine family there should be afflictions of such a Disciplinary character. The principle obtains in the education given by a wise earthly parent, who will prescribe tasks of more than usual difficulty and labour to a faithful and unreprovable child, for strengthening his endurance and improving his other virtues, with the view of qualifying him for administering the heritage he designs for him. The great Locke inculcates it as a first principle of education; and can we doubt that it obtains in the Education given by the Heavenly Father?

Secondly, it seems necessary to understand the *Paideia*, as it is expressed in the original—the *child-training* of the twelfth chapter of the epistle to the Hebrews, as including such Discipline for improving what is already good, as well as chastisement for correcting what is evil. The inculcation of Patience commences with referring the sufferers to the example of Christ, whose afflictions no one will represent as having been corrective of any personal fault. And what mean these words, "Though He were a Son, yet learned He obedience by the things which He suffered; and being made perfect, He became the author of eternal salvation unto all them that obey Him?" (Heb. v. 8, 9—compare ii. 10.) That the principal design of Christ's sufferings was the expiation of the sins of the guilty, I do not dispute but zealously contend. Nevertheless, in the course of accomplishing this object, his human nature, which "grew, and waxed strong in spirit" (Luke ii. 40) underwent a discipline not of *correction*, certainly, but of *sublimation*, so as to be made *perfect*,—not in the sense of being freed from any defect, but of being raised to consummate excellence, as the Lamb of God—not only white and spotless, but bright in the splendour of holiness.—It does not affect our present object much, though instead of the *perfection* being referred (as I think rightly) to the excellence of his *sacrifice*, it should be referred to his qualification for being a *sympathising* High Priest— from his having learned by experience (not to be obedient, but) what obedience *is*—what it costs—how difficult is its course even for the purest and holiest of natures, amid dangers and under afflictions. Even this interpretation represents his human nature as having been subjected to Discipline for its moral clevation. May not similar discipline be exercised over his followers?

Thirdly, the case of Abraham is pointedly illustrative. The *affliction* of the Patriarch is much overlooked; the attention being usually engrossed by the manner in which his Faith overcame all objections. But excepting that of Gethsemane it may be questioned if human nature was ever subjected to such agony as that which the Father of the Faithful suffered. From the time he received the commandment to sacrifice the son of his delight and hopes till it was revoked, Isaac was as much as dead to him. (Heb. xi. 19.) But this was as nothing. It was a three days' and wakeful nights' protracted, bloody immolation of him, by his own hand! Even with all his faith, that after the immolation he would recover him alive, somehow or other, sooner or later—likely just as he was dying, to be his heir—his anguish must have been inexpressible. Well, was all this torment inflicted on Abraham with a measure of divine displeasure, as a chastisement of sin? On the contrary, he was by this time highly spiritualised; having improved under former trials, and been cleared of blemishes which marred the beauty and dignity of his character, when his faith was young and comparatively raw. Some say there must have been the remains of corrupt nature in him, which, howsoever small, made him a fit subject for chastisement, that they might be *reduced*, though their extinction was hopeless. John Wesley, among many friends whom no one may despise for want either of sanctity or learning or power in the Protestant Church, replies that this imputation to Abraham of needfulness of chastisement, proceeds on a principle which he denounces as irrational and unscriptural, and something worse, viz., that God issues a commandment, "Be ye perfect," for the fulfilling of which He has made no provision—that his Spirit never chooses to aid the most importunate saint that length, and purposely restrains grace, so as to leave more or less sinfulness of which he may be divested at the moment of death, before the spirit enter into the heavenly kingdom. In opposition to this, Wesley and his friends contend that it is possible for a saint to attain in this world to the perfection commanded—and through the aid of the Spirit, proffered, yea pressed on his reception, to regain that state in which Adam was before he fell—sinless though liable to sin. Though not convinced, I am not able to answer their various arguments satisfactorily. The readiest and most common reply is to refer to 1 John i. 8, "If we say that we have no sin, we deceive ourselves." But Wesley replies, that in the remembrance of former sins there is enough of reason for a saint humbly confessing that he is a sinful person, though he is now free of evil habits and inclinations. There are many interpretations of scripture which pass unchallenged, not so specious as this.

But it is not requisite to take Wesley's ground in order to be consistent in maintaining that Abraham's affliction was not of the character of a chastisement. I observe, *first* of all, that, at the worst, the remains in him of original corrupt nature were small, and that God never *chastises* heavily, if at all, the slighter sins of his children, but corrects them by the remonstrances of his Spirit; and that it needs that sins be great and that evil habits be growing strong, or have grown inveterate, before He be provoked, yea, in mercy prevailed with, to scourge with the Rod. Calvin, in controverting the Popish doctrine of satisfaction, instances the case of Peter, who, though guilty of a heinous sin, was not chastised for it in any degree, because he was not obdurate and presently repented. (Institutes, B. iii., c. iv., sec. 35.) But why *speculate* thus on the case of Abraham? I observe, *secondly*, that we have the express declaration of the scripture that this particular affliction was not a chastisement, but a trial—not corrective but probative. (Gen. xxii. 1.) All agree that the rendering of the authorised version is unhappy, and that the proper one is, "God tried Abraham"—that is, *proved* him, or put him to the proof. No one can imagine that this means that the Lord, doubtful of the genuineness of the Patriarch's profession, or at least of the strength of his faith, made this crucial experiment on him for ascertaining its condition. This would have been as if a foolish and not very tender father, curious to know if he had been successful in the athletic exercising of his child, should lay a narrow plank over the flooded stream, and command him to walk across at the peril of being drowned. The Lord did, indeed, lay a narrow plank over the dreadful gulph for Abraham's crossing; but He knew, with certainty, that his favourite saint would both obediently and successfully perform the feat. What then was the object of this putting of him to the proof? I do not dispute that part of the design was to display him as an example to the world, and also to justify his government in the sight of men, in exalting to honour so great, one so eminent in piety. But this answer is insufficient. The requirements of the case are satisfied only by the explanation that the main design was to *strengthen* the faith by *exercising* it on a great task—to *prove* it in order to *improve* it; and this again in order to enhance the glory of the reward. Accordingly the angel—the Angel of the covenant, who can doubt?—well pleased with the display which his predestined father, according to the flesh, had made of his heroic faith, reiterated the promise with an exuberance of blessing.

There are several other declarations of scripture and recorded cases of saints by which the distinction between corrective and probative afflictions is approved; but because some of these will present themselves when illustrating the next distinction, I will close the illustration of the present with a practical application and appeal.—Afflicted one! It may be, for aught I know, that your sorrows are divinely permitted or commissioned for the corrective chastisement of evil habits and backslidings. Very possibly a part of their design at least is to quicken you into animation and vigour of spiritual life, out of a state of langour or lethargy into which you may have subsided. Even under such considerations of being *corrected*, it would be your duty to be thankfully resigned—being "chastened of the Lord, that you should not be condemned with the world." (1 Cor. xi. 32.) But, if after a short time's review of your life and introspection of your heart no evil habit or disposition is detected, of such magnitude as might account for your affliction, as a *fatherly* correction; and if on the contrary you are conscious of the genuineness of what Christian friends regard as an exemplary diligence in cultivating the graces of Christian life, I counsel you to give up the search for sins which may have incurred *chastisement*, and to turn your meditations to the possibility of its being the Lord's design to *prevent* some greater evil, or perhaps to *prepare* the way for some great advantage. This will facilitate your exercise of resignation. But, O! if there be any room for it, occupy it—the entertainment of the hope, that like Abraham you are *proved*, in order to be *improved*, so as to be qualified for a crown of special splendour. How easy then will be the exercise of resignation, under your affliction, howsoever painful! I have already said that it is few to whom this great consolation belongs; but more are entitled to it than apprehend it. There is on the part of some an unbelieving, unthankful, spurious modesty, akin to self-righteousness, which suppresses the feelings expressed by the apostle, when he says, "By the grace of God I am what I am." You may be one of the favourite few, who if they gave that grace its rightful acknowledgment would be sustained and animated under affliction by the hope of grace after grace, and reward surpassing reward. Moderate, at least, your self-jealousy: treat yourself with candour: yea, give the Spirit of God due credit for what He has wrought on you: yea, beware of doing dishonour to the Fatherhood of God, that when you are conscious of so much faithfulness, and with all your self-searchings for what is wrong can detect only some hastiness of temper, for instance, you should ascribe to this your sore affliction, with which in displeasure He *chastises* you! O, sin and shame! What a father of sternness you imagine Him to be? Change that way of speaking, and with it the feeling. He is not *chastising*, He is *proving* you, "that the trial of your faith, being much more precious than of gold that perisheth, though it be tried with fire, might be found unto (your) praise and honour and glory at the appearing of Jesus Christ." (1 Peter i. 7.)

FIFTH.—There are afflictions *Vicarious*:—I use the term *vicarious* reluctantly, and only from want of being prepared with a better. I deprecate being understood as using it in the sense in which it is commonly used of the sufferings of Christ when, substituted for the guilty, He bore the penalty of their sin. At present I merely express by it those afflictions to which the saint may be subjected—not for the correction, nor primarily for the profiting in any way of himself—but for the correction or profiting of others; and for which he will be compensated in the kingdom of his Father.—To this class also properly belong those afflictions in which he, though innocent, is involved in the course of the correction of those with whom he is associated in life—national judgments, for instance, or his father's bankruptcy—and for which too he shall have his compensation. It is those of the first character, however, with which the following illustrations will be almost exclusively engaged.

I commence with an imagined case, and yet so little imaginary that it is nearly the picture of one in real life; and its principal elements are not of uncommon occurrence. It is that of one who was a prosperous merchant, and not less a devout and liberal and in all respects an exemplary Christian. But notwithstanding all his parental care in their training, his two sons were growing up thriftless and dissipated, and his two daughters frivolous and fond of gaiety. They say it was his anxiety on this account which occasioned his disease. But that was not it. It was the hand of the Lord for the correction of his children. He was prostrated with apoplexy, and awoke from its stupor paralysed and incapacitated for life. His business was nearly wrecked; but the design was accomplished. His sons and daughters awoke from their stupor, too; but it was to lives of activity and eminence in piety and benevolence. The paralytic father, beholding the result, said, How dare I, how can I, complain of my affliction when it appears so evident that the Lord designed by it to save my children? *Your* children! I answered him; They are much more God's children than yours: and think you that He will take profit out of your afflictions for *his* family without largely compensating you? Learn, friend, to calculate your profits to better purpose. There *may have been* in your affliction the design of destroying some nascent in-creeping sin which escaped your own observation, or the prevention of some impending evil which only the Lord could foresee. A thought of even such possibilities will help your resignation. But independently of this there are these certainties—the reward of your patience—the reward consequent on your being more spiritualized by the Discipline—the reward which you enjoy of parental gratification in seeing those so dear to you, when regarded as your children, redeemed from their follies and sins, and made such a sweetness of heart to you by their filial sympathy and attentions, instead of threatening to be such a bitterness—such a praise to you, instead of threatening to be such a shame—the reward of meeting with them in the kingdom, they and you glorified together—but especially the reward of *your martyrdom*, as I hesitate not to call it, when those for whose interests you have suffered are regarded as being God's children—yea the martyr's reward for the benefit of which that suffering has been to the Church and the whole community; as having been used by the Lord as the means of that conversion of your sons and daughters in which such a fountain of public advantage was opened. What compensations! my afflicted friend. Instead of the thought of them producing merely an unmurmuring and acquiescent submission, it might loose your paralysed and stammering tongue, and make you sing for thanksgiving, not only in the midst of your tribulation, but *for* it, singing Welcome Suffering!—He said, Amen.

As a case of scriptural authority, that of the Father of the Faithful was of good avail for illustration, under the immediately preceding topic; that of his son both according to the flesh and the spirit, the Apostle of the Gentiles, will avail us equally well under the present.— Paul had one of the most afflicted lives which the Providence of God ever allotted to a saint; and the question at present is, Of what character were those afflictions, in respect of God's design in appointing them? The vague and vulgar answer of course is, that they were of the character of *chastisements* for the reducing of the remains of sin. Now, although Paul frequently appeals to the churches as witnesses of his integrity and blamelessness, and confident in his uprightness calls on them to make him their example; and in the retrospect of his Christian career says at its close, " I have fought a good fight, I have finished my course, I have kept the faith: henceforth there is laid up for me a crown of righteousness"—nevertheless, I doubt not that even after his conversion there were in him remains of sin; nor that the intent of his afflictions was in a degree and subordinately a correction of these remains. But here is my contention : that Paul himself, notwithstanding all the free and open manner in which he reveals to us the state of his heart and life, *never once*, after undergoing the horrors of his chastisement at his conversion, speaks of his sufferings as being corrective of any sin. When at 2 Cor. vi. 9 he represents himself, according to the authorised version, as being "chastened," all scholars know that the term in the original (παιδευομενοι not μαστιγομενοι) is the generic term for Discipline, and does not necessarily imply chastisement.—The "thorn in the flesh" of which he speaks at 2 Cor. xii. 7, whatever it may particularly mean, denotes only a *preventive* affliction; preventive of pride incident to his favoured case. He himself expressly says so. (What lack there is of common sense among many in not distinguishing betwixt sin, and susceptibility of temptation to sin! Adam in innocence was susceptible.) His "keeping his body under," of which he speaks at 1 Cor. ix. 27, indicates neither divine chastisement, nor even the existence of sin to be chastised by self-inflicted penance. These are all the instances I have observed which even an inaccurate judgment may construe as descriptive of corrective *chastisements*.

It is somewhat different with the representation of his afflictions being of that Disciplinary, probative character which has been previously explained. That the whole of his afflictions contributed to this end is undoubted; and that they were partly designed for it may be argued from 2 Cor. vi. 9, already quoted. But this is not to the point, the question being, Were these afflictions, in respect of their design by God, entirely of a corrective, preventive, preparative or probative character? I answer, that with the exception of the "thorn in the flesh," which was *preventive*, they were neither wholly nor principally of one or other of these characters; and that but for a different design the greater part of them at least would never have been inflicted: that primarily and chiefly they had not respect to Paul's personal advantage, but were designed for the advantage of others; that is, were of a *vicarious* character, in the sense already explained.

The key of interpretation is found in the mission of Ananias to Paul, when the days of his dark chastisement were accomplished: "Go thy way: for he is a chosen vessel unto Me, to bear my name before the Gentiles, and kings, and the children of Israel. For I will show him how great things he must suffer for my name's sake." (Acts ix. 15, 16.) With the two slight exceptions already noticed, this vicariousness is uniformly the character which Paul throughout his epistles ascribes to his many and heavy afflictions. His declaration, made at 2 Tim. ii. 10, is perhaps the most emphatic and comprehensive: "Therefore I endure all things for the elect's sakes, that they may also obtain the salvation which is in Christ Jesus with eternal glory." But I select for particular examination his statements and representations occurring in the fourth chapter of the second epistle to the Corinthians; not only on account of their evidence for that which I at present especially plead, but on account of the opportunity which their examination will afford for correcting mistakes and establishing the truth on some other subjects within the general scope of these illustrations. I premise that I regard the "we" and "our" of the passage as used by a common figure of grammar for "I" and "my." Even in a parallel passage (1 Cor. iv. 9) where he commences with the expression, "us, the apostles," he presently proceeds, in defence of his apostleship which had been impunged by false teachers at Corinth, with an account of what was peculiarly his own experience. It is not a matter of much consequence, but the concentrating of our attentions on his case will facilitate the illustration.

2 CORINTHIANS, chapter iv. In verses 8-10 he gives a succinct account of his afflictions: "We are troubled on every side, yet not distressed; we are perplexed, but not in despair; persecuted, but not forsaken; cast down, but not destroyed; always bearing about in the body the dying of the Lord Jesus."—At verse 15th, he says that to all this he was subjected for their benefit: "For all things are for your sakes, that the abundant grace might, through the thanksgiving of many, redound to the glory of God." By this spiritual profiting on their part he was no doubt much gratified; but there was another consideration by which his heart was sustained, so that he fainted not, viz., the prospect of being largely compensated for all the afflictions, when " He who raised up the Lord Jesus shall raise us up also by Jesus" (v. 14.) And at verse 17th, he breaks out in these exultant strains: "For our light affliction, which is but for a moment, worketh for us a far more exceeding and eternal weight of glory; while we look not at the things which are seen, but at the things which are not seen: for the things which are seen are temporal; but the things which are not seen are eternal."

After the illustrations made of both corrective and probative afflictions, I cannot be justly accused of undervaluing their importance; but I contend that the idea of neither of them is contained in the whole of the passage; and though many both impressive and profitable sermons have been preached with verse 17th as a text, illustrative of the efficacy and benefit of affliction in general, in correcting sin and promoting spirituality, that its scope has been misapprehended. The affliction referred to is specially that of the apostle described in the context; and *the working*, or as it would be better rendered, *working out* ($\chi\alpha\tau\epsilon\rho\gamma\alpha\zeta\epsilon\tau\alpha\iota$) of a result ascribed to it, is not the producing of an improved state of mind and character. That this was one of the results is doubtless; but it is not the one referred to in the text, where it is explicitly stated to be "glory." The apostle evidently designs to express a contrast; but there is no proper contrast betwixt antecedent affliction and consequent spiritualization; whereas "glory" contrasts strictly with "afflictions:"—the "weight" of the one, with the "lightness" of the other—and the "eternal duration" of the one with the other's "momentariness." What, now, is more particularly the "glory" which the afflictions work out? Evidently that spoken of at verse 14th, to be revealed at the Resurrection of the just.—And how does the affliction work it out? I answer, Not by the mediation of a moral *meetness* for glory which it influences, but *directly* as securing it in the way of a compensatory reward—"far more exceeding in weight" the antecedent labour; it is of *grace*, truly; but still it is a reward of service. No one denies the production of moral meetness, and I, for one, believe that that will *increase* the glory; but I equally maintain that it is not referred to in the present text; and that the afflictions are represented as working out the glory irrespectively of it; it being of course understood that a meetness is acquired both through these afflictions and many other means. If anything more be required to make the demonstration of the point clear, it will be found at the conclusion of the apostle's testimony to the hope by which he was inspired: "While we look not at the things which are seen, but at the things which are not seen." The "look" does not express one of mere sanctifying contemplation; but one of *aim*, and calculating respect to advantages. And the particle "while" connects "the things not seen" with the "weight of glory," in comparison with which "the things which are seen," whether painful or pleasurable, threatening or promising, are unworthy of regard. The case of Paul, then, is distinctly this, that he fainted not, through having, like Moses, " respect unto the recompense of the reward" for the many and great afflictions to which he was vicariously subjected for the church's sake.

The case of Paul furnishes a principle for the illustration of the cases of all martyrs, or of those who are persecuted for teaching the Truth—of missionaries—of not a few ministers of the Gospel at home, labouring assiduously amid privations, when their talents and acquirements would have raised them to wealth and honourable estate in worldly business and professions —of Christian patriots who have suffered in fortune, character, and person in the cause of civil liberty—of pious physicians, than whose profession no other furnishes more examples of benevolent unrequited labour —of pious philanthropists, men and women, who have made themselves poor, or keep themselves poor, by their attentions and ministrations of charity for the relief of the indigent, the education of the ignorant, and the reclaiming of the vicious. The suffering, toil, expenditure, and self-denial of those and all such fall to be classed as vicarious, and rewarded as such. And be it observed, that this character is ascribable to sufferings and privations and acts of self-denial, not only when the work on behalf of others is *imposed*, so to speak, on the sufferers by special providences, which shut them up to the work, or by peculiar impulses of the Spirit, as has been the experience of not a few of our best missionaries; but when it is purely spontaneously, and without any special excitement, that the well-doers will turn off from the common highway of a respectable dutifulness, and enter the wilderness,—as when the merchant, liberal in pious and charitable contributions, shall deny himself to the solicitations of evening festivities, and take his usual walk of relaxation from business down the Vennel to visit the wretched, and die of the pestilential infection; yea, without the martyrdom of dying, will he not be rewarded for his *self-denial?* Will it be all the same in that day for him and the banqueters? I do not condemn the banqueters—it may be quite lawfully that they enjoy themselves. My appeal is on behalf of him who is away down the Vennel, when they are feasting, that he be awarded a higher place of honour than theirs in the heavenly kingdom.—The old impure legalism! some will exclaim. The old heresy that condemns it! I rejoin; which involves in its profane censure Him who taught, exhorted, and promised thus—" When thou makest a feast, call the poor, the maimed, the lame, the blind: and thou shalt be blessed; for they cannot recompense thee: for thou shalt be *recompensed* at the resurrection of the just." (Luke xiv. 13, 14.)

The various ends of mercy which God intends by the affliction of his children having been reviewed, a question of great importance presses, which cannot but have often occurred in the course of the illustration to the minds of the reflective, but which, though it has not been entirely unnoticed, could not receive such extended treatment as it requires, till the whole field of affliction had been surveyed. Even yet I cannot promise a satisfactory answer, but only the clearing of the subject of a few misconceptions; the question is so subtle, through referring to such delicate shades of feeling. It is not, If it be obligatory on a Christian, after he has passed through a trial, and experiences or sees the profitable results, to be grateful that he was subjected to it; neither is it, If it be his duty, when under the pressure of the affliction, to be persuaded that its design is merciful, and that the result will be profitable, so as to be unmurmuringly and acquiescently submissive;—Here is the question, Is it his duty to *welcome* the affliction when it visits him—to be *cheerful* under it—and *glad* for its prolongation?

Although there occurs, both in public sermons and private exhortations, not a little indiscretion (to express the censure lightly) in inculcating such *gladness* as a duty, yet it cannot be denied, notwithstanding the mocking of some at what they call the fantasticalness of the question, that such a state of mind is reasonably attainable: reasonably, I say, without fanciful excitement, and in the order of a calm and sound faith.— Will not the diseased man eagerly lay hold on the extended medicinal cup, and how bitter and nauseous soever the contents, drain it gladly through hope of relief? And will not that company of the beleaguring armament, whom the general has selected for entering the breach, when they receive the intelligence, raise a shout of exultation; and, animated by the honour of the preference, the hope of posthumous fame or of promotion in the ranks, and by the patriotic spirit of quelling the enemy, rush into the jaws of almost certain death? A veteran who had thrice *volunteered* for making the dreadful pass, complained to me that people should call it the *forlorn hope;* for that in all his long campaigning he had never felt so *magnificently* (as he expressed himself) as when on those three occasions he advanced into the breach. When in such cases we have instances of men being glad for what is painful or dangerous, under the influence of worldly motives, why should it be thought unreasonable or fantastical that other men should be as glad, under the influence of spiritual motives? The apostles, after being beaten and threatened, " departed from the presence of the council, rejoicing that they were counted worthy to suffer shame for His name." (Acts v. 41.) And Paul warmly felicitates the Philippians, that unto them " it is given (not appointed merely, but given as a favour) in the behalf of Christ, not only to believe on Him, but also to suffer for his sake." (Philip. i. 29.) And he eulogises the Hebrew Christians, saying, " Ye took joyfully the spoiling of your goods, knowing in yourselves that ye have in heaven a better and an enduring substance, [compared with what is lost, and in compensation of the loss]." (Heb. x. 34.)

But it is the case of Paul himself which, as on a previous occasion, furnishes us with the most striking illustration: "*Most gladly* therefore," he exclaims, " will I rather glory in my infirmities, that the power of Christ may rest upon me: Therefore I *take pleasure* in infirmities, in reproaches, in necessities, in persecutions, in distresses for Christ's sake: for when I am weak, then am I strong." (2 Cor. xii. 9, 10.) Nothing can surpass this in spiritual beauty and venerableness. But for that very reason, how inconsiderate it is, yea, how cruel, how significant of the wrong-doer's ignorance and want of personal experience, when any one, minister, elder, or private friend shall, on a visit of condolence, take up the experience and example of one who, through long and peculiar discipline, and special endowment of the Comforter for his arduous work, had attained to an elevation of spiritual and heavenly mindedness rarely if ever equalled in the history of the Church,—and apply it, yea, perversely misapply it, for the rebuke of the sufferer's tears and lamentations; saying that, like Paul, he should rather be *glad* for his afflictions, and *take pleasure* in them, as being fatherly chastisements and evidences of his adoption, and that to mourn *that way*, shows a sinful weakness of faith, against which he should engage much in prayer!—It is not a little of such barbarity which is perpetrated under the pretence of Christian sympathising. The farthest that Paul's example can be legitimately urged is to employ it in the way of encouragement, as an illustration of the great height of consolation, to which faith, well exercised, can lift up the heart: but never to make it a test of the genuineness either of our own feelings and principles or those of our friends. All that is imperative, and that may be exacted as evidence of a dutiful state of mind, is "patience in tribulation," with which *mourning* as contradistinguished from *murmuring*, is quite compatible. Heretofore I have noticed (page 104) this old favourite distinction, and with the slight qualification then made renew my recommendation of it. I have known many instances of its benefit. Observe how Paul sanctions it. He does not set up his own peculiar experience as a standard by which to measure others; so as to condemn them if they have not attained to his stature. His general maxim for the regulation of the feelings of the Church is this,—"No chastening for the present seemeth to be joyous, but grievous"—such is the permission of *mourning:* "nevertheless afterward it yieldeth the peaceable fruit of righteousness"—such is the prohibition of *murmuring.* (Heb. xii. 11.) I do not murmur, said a sorely-tried friend, for I am fully persuaded that all these afflictions are mercifully intended; but oh that the Lord had seen some other way less grievous than this for effecting his purpose! Some may be ready to question if this was Resignation; but One before him had said, "O my Father! if it be possible, let this cup pass from me." Thrice he prayed thus, "with strong crying and tears." (Matthew xxvi. 39; Heb. v. 7.)

"Looking unto Jesus," is the great exemplar law. (Heb. xii. 2.) In the way of accommodation, the words may be employed to express dependance on Him in all our exigences and expectations, and obedience to Him in all our work. But as used by the apostle in the text they are restricted to the contemplation, imitation, and following of Him as the Exemplar of Faith, "in running with patience the race set before us"—the Model Practiser and Fulfiller of Faith in his own conduct—the Chief of the Cloud of Witnesses.—When the Common Translation, in which the word "our" is supplied without authority, represents Him as being "the Author and Finisher of *our* Faith," in the sense of being the communicator of it to others, and the rearer of it into strength, or at last its rewarder,—

though this is all true, as declared elsewhere, yet even those who are not scholars might suspect that it cannot be the meaning here: for it harmonises imperfectly with the preceding context, and is discordant with the subsequent, which, in illustration of the title given Him, proceeds with an account, not of his official action, but of his personal conduct. The old interpretation dislocates the whole passage; the other preserves its complete unity. Accordingly, all scholars agree that the word of the original translated in our version *author*, denotes a *leader*, and the greater part understand that translated *finisher* in the sense of his *perfecting* the exercise of faith in his own endurance of affliction.

Looking unto Jesus, as our Exemplar in the exercise of Faith! I rejoice greatly in the interpretation. I find enough elsewhere of commandment to make his example of prayerfulness, of humility, of purity, of charity, and of zeal for the truth, the law of life. But when I have here the commandment to take Him for my Exemplar in his character of a *believer*, then am I much relieved from suspicions of the genuineness of my own faith; for I see that his perfect faith admitted of agonised, deprecatory praying, "with strong crying and tears," under the pressure of affliction; and I counsel any brother in sorrow that if, in the confidence of faith, he commence like Christ with "O my Father!" and, in the submission of Faith, conclude as He did, with " Nevertheless not as I will, but as Thou wilt," then he need not restrain himself in filling up the interval with whatever expressions of lamentation he may feel nature requires for giving vent to his grief.

Having determined what is the Exemplar law, I might conclude here without adverting to a difficulty which no doubt presents itself to some minds; because that difficulty, though unexplained, could not affect the force of the law. However, the question being not only interesting in Christology generally, but one the elucidation of which will contribute to confirm the particular views which have just been propounded, I shall give a place to its consideration. The difficulty is this:—Do not the foregoing illustrations tend to produce the impression that Paul carried the virtue of fortitude under sufferings higher than Christ did? No Socinian can on his own principles deny it; nor need he, in order to be consistent as an impugner of the doctrine of sacrificial atonement. We will have full proof of this as we proceed with resolving the difficulty.

Observe, then, First, that Christ's agony that night in Gethsemane was a peculiar incident in his life; and that He who delighted to do his Father's will, and had such clear faith in the glory which should follow his term of humiliation, must have borne afflictions generally with great equanimity, and little sensitiveness to worldly privations and pains. On the other side, Paul, though never in a murmuring, was not always in a joyous frame of mind. Of this there is abundant evidence throughout his epistles. And when in writing to the Corinthians he speaks of himself, as being "glad" for his afflictions, and as taking "pleasure" in them, not only should we take into consideration the excitement and warmth of expression of friendly correspondence, but the circumstance that he is for the time being enjoying at Ephesus comparative repose; and in the retrospect of the advantage of which his past afflictions had been both to himself and the church, and calculating for the future by the same measure, he rejoices for the life of trouble which was appointed him. But does not Christ also rejoice now in the retrospect of the agony He endured in Gethsemane?

Observe, Secondly, that Christ was ordained to mental suffering. "Travail of soul" was a constituent element of his expiation of our sins. Besides; the impartation to his human nature of a large measure of comfort would have reduced the atoning value of his bodily sufferings, by rendering Him to a great extent insensible to them. He would not have been manifested the Man of Sorrows—a manifestation needful in the eyes of angels and men for the justification of the Divine government in the method of our salvation. (Rom. iii. 26.) Hence the communication of comfort was nearly restrained to the point of *sustaining* Him, so that he might not sink under his burden. His whole course on earth, with but little exception, shows this:—The triumphant scene of his entry into Jerusalem, amid the Hosannas of the multitude and the children, was short-lived; and lasted only so long as was necessary to enter protest for and take enfeoffment (Scotticè *infeftment*) of his royal rights.—The

Transfiguration glory was also evanescent, and bestowed principally for sustaining Him under approaching trials —And his "rejoicing in spirit," mentioned at Luke x. 21, is recorded as something uncommon in his life of sorrow.—On the other side, though Paul likewise was ordained to great bodily afflictions (Acts ix. 16), there was equally provided for him an extraordinary bestowment of mental happiness—not only for *sustaining* him, but making him buoyant in spirit, defiant of dangers, and triumphant in distress. "And when they had laid many stripes upon them, they cast them into prison, and made their feet fast in the stocks. And at midnight Paul and Silas prayed and *sang praises unto God:* and the prisoners heard them." (Acts xvi. 23-25.) The working out of our salvation did not admit of such *joyousness* for *Him*, who hath "borne our griefs and carried our sorrows."

Observe, therefore, Thirdly, that Christ's sorrow was the procuring cause of Paul's joy. Not only did that sorrow of Christ, as a constituent element of his work in the expiation of sin, gain for Paul the *ground* of his joy as a pardoned man, but the *feeling of joy* itself as a communication of the Comforter. Nor was this all; the gifts of the Spirit, gained by the sacrifice of Christ, are *dispensed* according to his intercession, and by his mediatorial authority; and it is to our purpose to remark, that when at Philippians iv. 13, Paul says, "I can do all things through *Christ* which strengtheneth me," he refers especially to the manner in which He sustains him in a contented and cheerful state of mind under all his privations.

Surely enough has been produced in the way of argument to place the Master and the servant in their proper places. But there is another matter which it will be profitable to consider, not only as being confirmatory of the point at present more immediately before us, but as being of itself of the greatest interest and importance.

I appeal, therefore, Fourthly, What were Paul's sufferings for which he rejoiced, compared with those of Christ which educed his tears and cries and deprecatory supplications?—In the course of the preceding illustrations several popular errors both in doctrine and practice have come in the way to excite censure and reprobation; but here we meet with what verily *amazes* me—representations made by men pious, learned, and judicious, which I do not hesitate to accuse of being deeply dishonourable to the personal character of our Lord, and as at one blow demolishing the doctrine of his sacrificial atonement, and this, too, when the resolution of the difficulty, if difficulty there be, lies on the surface. This is a heavy charge: let readers judge of its equity.

The reply which those with whom I now most reluctantly contend make to the question, or rather exclamation, What were Paul's sufferings compared with those of Christ! is virtually that they were no less, or rather much the same; that death threatened them both in forms equally fearful—in the case of Christ in the form of being crucified, for the gratification of the malice of Jewish Priests; in that of Paul, in the form of being beheaded for the gratification of the bloodthirstiness of Nero; but that Paul, in the immediate prospect of *his* death, was composed, yea triumphant, saying, " I am now ready to be offered; henceforth there is laid up for me a crown of righteousness;" whereas Christ, in the prospect of *his*, was agonised with terror, and prayed importunately to be saved from it, if possible. It is painful to write, and I hope painful for many to read, what is so discrediting to our Lord.

When those who make the injurious representation explain that it was not a common crucifixion which He deprecated, but one of peculiar horror; because in it He would be subjected to the bearing of the curse of the sin of the whole world, or at least of the whole elect part of it, What, I ask, do they mean ? Is it that He feared that scope would be given to the malice of the Priests, the prototypes of Popish Inquisitors, in refining, somehow or other, the torture of crucifixion? Or, that He feared that Divine Justice might demand more than an ordinary prolongation of suffering, and for that end might supernaturally sustain Him in life, under more agony than the human constitution usually requires for its extinction ? I do not ask such questions with the least of a feeling of burlesque. Both the cause, and the character of the men whom I question forbid this. Let them tell us something, though it be ever so general and undefined, of the reason wherefore Christ was agonised in the prospect of death, when Paul was composed. It is no answer to say, that the *causes* of the deaths were different, and that the cause of that of

Christ, being the weightier, it gave reason to apprehend a more dreadful issue; for there was no room for imagining fears: both of the deaths were distinctly specified, and they were equally dreadful. I therefore repeat the demand, Will they give us any plausible explanation which sustains the honour of our great Exemplar—of Paul encountering *his* death with little or no perturbation of mind, when Christ anticipated *his* with a fear which produced perspiration of blood? They never will, so long as they imagine that it was the fear of crucifixion by which Christ was agonised in Gethsemane.

But, dismissing all comparison with the case of Paul, I go on to remark that, how much soever they may magnify Christ's reasons for regarding the Cross in such near prospect with horror, the fact will remain, that according to their views He prayed for deliverance from drinking the prepared cup of that Cross's anguish, if it were possible. It is this that *amazes* me especially, in the teaching of pious and learned men. Observe, they admit that, whether through the illumination of his own Divine nature, or that of the Spirit of his Father, the human soul of Christ was clearly convinced that in order to the fulfilment of his mission He must suffer a violent death, and that specially by being "lifted up" on the Cross; and yet they represent Him as praying that He might be delivered from it if possible. Is not this amazing interpretation indeed? —to represent Him praying for that, as being possibly possible, which He was sure was impossible—for that as being possibly agreeable to his Father's will, the contrary of which He knew his Father's will had from eternity decreed—for that which, were it granted, He distinctly knew would be a complete abandonment of the enterprise of the world's salvation? The amazement is only heightened by the attempted explanation. It is, that the natural shrinking of Christ's humanity, in view of the impending sufferings of crucifixion, prevailed *for a moment* to make Him pray for deliverance; but that He presently recovered his fortitude! Now, though this alleged succumbing to natural fear had been momentary, which it was not—for He prayed in the same manner a second and a third time at considerable intervals—though it had been strictly momentary, what could have been said in justification of the feelings and expressions of that moment? To represent the human nature of Christ as *shrinking* in the near view of that cross of torment discredits neither his fortitude nor faith. It would not increase my admiration of the character of Paul to be assured that he did not *shrink* at the sight of the headsman with his axe; but it is one thing to shrink in the sight of impending suffering and utter exclamations of woe, and quite another to desire an escape when duty clearly demands submission to it; and something very different to pray to be delivered from it, when he who prays knows that deliverance is impossible. Yet, this is what many represent Christ to have done. I may not mention in connection with his Name what this imputes to Him. I only say it is amazing that "in the house of his friends," He should be wounded by the imputation.

The amazement rises yet higher, when the difficulty, if difficulty there be in the case, is so easily explained. I therefore vehemently, and on behalf of Christ, indignantly deny that his prayer was either momentarily or conditionally deprecatory of his being made to drink to-morrow of the prepared cup of the expiatory sufferings of the cross; and contend that it was deprecatory only of the prolongation of his drinking of that cup of *mental anguish* which was already, that dark night, being administered to Him. What were all the ingredients of that cup no man may attempt satisfactorily to explain. That horror of the cross was one of them is most probable; but if so it was not the cross from which He prayed to be delivered, but the present overwhelming horror of it.

Independently of direction from any other quarter we might have concluded, with certainty, from the evangelical narratives themselves that it was the cup of *mental tribulation* which He was presently drinking, that was the object of his deprecatory prayer. I, for one, could not for a moment have entertained the imagination (to be afterwards dispossessed of it), that when He was yet warm, so to speak, from instituting an ordinance to be observed by his church in all ages till he returned in his glory, as commemorative of his approaching death, He should yet have commenced to pray for escape from that death, with strong crying and tears; and that, too, after having mocked at Peter's self-confidence, when he protested that he would not succumb, even momentarily, to the natural shrinking from death. But without any such prepossession of mind against the possibility of the cross itself being the object of his deprecation, the narrative at its very commencement determines what the cup is, and discloses the Saviour drinking of it: " My soul is exceeding sorrowful, even unto death." It is this agony of *sorrow* which forms the subject of the whole passage—as being the contents of the cup—as being that from which He prayed to be delivered—and as being that from which He *was* delivered. To represent the agonies of the cross as being the contents of the deprecated cup is not only morally objectionable in the highest degree, but evinces a lack of exegetical scholarship, in substituting a supposed *cause* of the sorrow for the *sorrow* itself, which is pointedly set forth as the subject of the narrative,—a substitution which has produced, in the attempted expositions of those who make it, a jumble of self-contradictions, and what is worse, most injurious imputations to the character of our Lord.*

Although, however, there is enough in the evangelical narratives themselves of Matthew, Mark, and Luke, to convince us that the deprecated cup was that of present

---

* When our translators render Matt. xxvi. 39, "Let this cup pass *from* Me, not *by* Me, the rendering is supported by Schleusner, who translates *discedat a Me;* and in like manner with Mark xiv. 36, "Take away *from* Me :" and Luke xxii. 42, "Remove *from* Me," he translates *aufer a Me.* But in the present instance, at least, it is not as a grammarian I build anything on philological niceities, but, as a critic, appeal to the nature and whole scope of the case.

mental agony, and not that of the approaching pains of crucifixion, yet, when error prevails so much we cannot dispense with referring to the inspired testimony of the apostle as given in Heb. v. 7: "Who in the days of his flesh, when He had offered up prayers and supplications with strong crying and tears unto Him that was able to save Him from death; and was heard in that He feared."

In adducing this evidence we are, in the first instance, met by the denial of Macknight, that the apostle refers in these words to the scene of Gethsemane at all. His argument is, that whereas the apostle represents Him as having prayed for and received deliverance from *death*, He presented no such prayer that night; for this eminent critic contends as vehemently as I have done, that to suppose Him to have prayed in fear of the cross " would be to degrade his character infinitely." (Harmony, sect. cxxxiv.) He therefore "conjectures" that the praying with strong crying and tears, spoken of by Paul, refers to some incident in Christ's life which none of the evangelists have recorded; and of which the apostle was informed either by tradition or direct inspiration; and that his resurrection from the dead was that for which He prayed, and in which He was answered. Is not this strange conjecturing for one deservedly in high repute for his many excellences as an expositor, and worth whole colleges of German fancy-critics? What! No threatening of death in the Gethsemane scene, from which our Lord could pray to be delivered! when He began to be sorrowful, and very heavy, and sore amazed, and said "My soul is exceeding sorrowful, *even unto death*," and when He fell on his face praying in agony for deliverance, and when his sweat was as it were great drops of blood falling down to the ground! Even according to these expressions could death be more imminent? But Dr. Doddridge, with good cause, complains that "the words which our translators use here are very flat, and fall vastly short of the emphasis of these terms in which the evangelists describe the awful scene." Especially that translated "very heavy" signifies "overwhelmed with anguish." What greater nearness to death, through mental suffering, could any one reasonably demand to warrant applying to the case the words of the apostle, that He prayed for deliverance to Him who was able to "save from death?" Almost all other expositors express themselves to the effect that Christ must have felt as if He would die, were the mental agony prolonged. And Macknight himself says, "His human nature being now *burdened beyond measure*, He found it necessary to retire and pray, that if it was possible, or consistent with the salvation of the world, He might be delivered from the sufferings which were *then lying* on Him." (Harmony, sect. xxxiv.) I therefore dismiss the "conjecture" as unworthy of the honoured name of the dreamer—by few honoured so much as by him who laments and censures the temporary hallucination.

Having established what has been almost the universal opinion in all ages of the church that Heb. v. 7 refers to the scene in Gethsemane, on its authority

I argue, that Christ was delivered from *that death* which He deprecated; and that that could not be the prospective death of the cross, since He *was not* delivered from it, but the present imminent death, through mental agony, whatever may have been its causes, from which He *was* delivered. There is a difference among critics about the precise meaning of the words of the original, translated in the common version "was heard in that He feared." But all agree that they signify that his prayer was answered. It does not appear, but it does not much affect the great question, whether the apostle refers particularly to the mission of the angel to strengthen Him, (Luke xxii. 43), or generally to the manner in which his subsequent conduct indicated that He had been delivered from that anguish of soul, extruding bloody sweat, which made Him feel that He must presently die, unless He were relieved. Why, instead of deprecating the cross, He prayed that He might be spared for it.

My argument is properly concluded; but some might complain, if, after having demonstrated that it was the cup of mental agony of which he was drinking, for the removal of which our Lord prayed, I did not give some explanation of the nature and cause or causes of that agony. But no one without being guilty of presumption may attempt to elucidate that great mystery. I shall therefore only submit a few *notes* on the subject; and when their unsatisfactoriness is felt as a solution of the difficulty, be it observed that the obscurity occurs not less on the principles of those with whom I have been disputing, than on those for which I contend.

1st, It surely needs no more than a statement of it for making it be dismissed from consideration, when I note that one of the old modes of resolving the difficulty was to represent Divine Justice as having injected or immitted images of horror into the soul of Christ, in the course of his substitutionary sufferings for the guilty. Nor was it only of old, among those who are called the Primitive Fathers, that such a speculation obtained. Is it not another subject of *amazement*, that even Dr. Doddridge should express himself in favour of the notion, that "God by his own immediate agency impressed some uncommon horrors on His mind?" (Expositor clxxxii.)

2nd, Not only some of the ancient Fathers, but diverse divines of modern times, such as Grotius (Annot. Heb. v. 7), Hammond (Psal. xxii. 1), Macknight (Harm. cxxxiv.), account for the agony, by Christ's divine nature having for the time withdrawn its usual support from his human nature. This grotesque representation of Christ having momentarily deserted Himself, proceeds from erroneous views of the Incarnation, or as divines call it the Hypostatical union; in which, according to the Scripture, it was the Holy Spirit by whom the Eternal Father fashioned, qualified, and sustained a human nature, fitted for union with that of his Eternal Son. (See Appendix.)

3rd, Although the immediately preceding explanation

has been rejected, yet the grand principle of solving the difficulty is essentially contained in it—that principle being, that for wise ends in the economy of Redemption, there was a temporary diminution in the communication of *Divine aid* to the human nature; so that his soul was left, more than was usual, to its natural imaginings and emotions. This has been partly explained already in comparing the cases of Christ and Paul (page 143), and will be further illustrated in the Appendix. Meantime I remark that it cannot be consistently objected to by those who represent Him as having been temporarily so overcome by the natural fear of death, as to have prayed for that which in a self-possessed mood He knew it was impossible to grant Him. This implies an extent of Divine *desertion*, whether of his own Divinity, or of the Spirit of his Father, yea, of the Reason of his human nature, the imagination of which I repudiate with horror.

4th, Though the notion of Divine Justice having, "by its own immediate agency, impressed some uncommon horrors on His mind," has been dismissed with reprobation—that of the Great Tempter, having done so, seems most probable. It is said, that after the Temptation in the wilderness, "he departed from Him *for a season*," as if he should return to the assault. (Luke iv. 13.) Just before entering Gethsemane, He said "the Prince of this world cometh." (John xiv. 30.) And, to those who came to apprehend Him, He said "this is your hour and the *power of darkness*," Luke xxii. 53, in which latter expression, commentators generally think, reference is made to the agency of Satan; for whom it was the last opportunity he would have of tormenting our Lord, and which he would use to the utmost extent of his mysterious power, with his dark insinuations.

5th, Many divines have speculated that God in preparing a human nature for his Only Begotten Son (Heb. x. 5), fashioned it of peculiar excellence and high refinement, so as to be peculiarly sensitive, both bodily and mentally. I approve of this and have adopted it in the Appendix. But the speculation is not necessary for persuading any reflective person that it must have been in a very debilitated and enervated condition He entered Gethsemane, how robust soever his native constitution may have been. Even from early age till He entered on his public ministry, as the destined and separated Lamb of sacrifice, He must have passed a youthtime and manhood of depressing sorrow. Having entered on that ministry, to what a course He was subjected of three years' enfeebling labour, privation, reproach, danger, and varied anxiety! More especially, how exhausting and agitating had his labours and the occurrences been, during these eight days since He had come up to Jerusalem to the feast! More especially still, how painfully exciting these hours must have been of what has almost without a figure been characterised as His "death-bed arrangements and exhortations!" What then? Just what all who speak and write intelligently on the subject say; though it may be with the use of different phrases from those which I employ. And what is that? It is that Christ as the sacrificial victim of our sins, and in order to his being qualified at all points from personal experience to be a sympathetic High-Priest, was, when He entered Gethsemane that dark night, subjected for a season to the direst distress to which, excepting the agony of an accusing conscience, human nature is liable. And what again is that? I answer, *nervous debility*—with its universal gloom, its heaviness, its unrest, its sense of utter desolation — when even for saints of great eminence there will be nothing left but the *conviction of faith* in the Divine love, without any *sensible* experience of it, or any *manifestation* of it enjoyed by the soul. How widely does not this distress prevail! And is there no sympathy with it, from personal experience of its woe, on the part of Him of whom it is said, as one of his most endearing qualifications, "We have not an High-Priest which cannot be touched with the feeling of our *infirmities;* but was in all *points* tempted like as we are?" To make an exception of this form of distress, is to exclude his sympathy from the widest and darkest region of human misery. It would indeed be a profanity for any one to say that the whole, or even the chief part of the Gethsemane Act of our Lord's Passion is explicable on this principle: but equally it convicts a man of much incompetency for the office of being a helper of the Church's faith, when he ignores the principle. There is a great multitude, sound in faith and of tender conscience, who misconstrue these "darkenings of the flesh," (as the older divines described nervous depression of the spirits), as indicative of unbelief; so that their distress is greatly aggravated by the self-accusation: and that person is greatly wanting in the art of spiritual healing, who is not prepared to administer one of the most soothing elixirs of the gospel—that Christ, in whom there was no unbelief, suffered woefully from similar "darkenings of the flesh;" and that there is no affliction in which He more compassionately sympathises with his saints, from personal experience of the anguish of a spirit thus deeply, vitally wounded, "even unto death." The remembrance of it serves Him with sympathy even in that with which He cannot directly sympathise, but the pain of which is akin to it—the agony of a wounded conscience.

6th, It only remains that something, howsoever unsatisfactory, be noted respecting the *subjects* which may have engaged and exercised the mind of Christ, so as to occasion its state of agony.—Possibly, there was little definite in his meditations and reflections: and his state of mind may, to a great extent, have been such as sometimes befalls his saints, when they are oppressed with a sense of dismal desolation, of the reasons of which they cannot give any precise account. —Nevertheless, it could not well be that, in the circumstances, some objects calculated to excite the feelings painfully did not present themselves distinctly to our Lord's mind. *First*, though I have exerted myself to prove that Christ did not pray for deliverance from the Cross, yet I am persuaded that that *horror of mind*, for deliverance from which He did pray, was to a great extent occasioned by the near prospect of that death of anguish, with all its attendant circumstances of abuse, mockery, and shame. *Second*, in like manner, though I have shown that reflections on the evil of the world's sin, the curse of which He was about to bear, could not augment his fear, from his speculating that its avengement must be something uncommonly dreadful, since He knew distinctly what that avengement would be— the crucifixion common to malefactors, yet I object not to the representations in which some enlarge that the world's sin, as being the cause of his impending sufferings, must have presented itself to his mind with more than ordinary hideousness of aspect—"amazing" Him. *Third*, though Christ was assured that his own sufferings would be of short duration, and that He would soon "enter into his glory," the prospect of the sufferings of those endeared friends whom He left behind, and many more parties besides, must have affected Him deeply.

Having given a digest of the various opinions on this subject, its readers will acknowledge that I spoke very truly when I said at the commencement that I would not give them satisfaction. Enough, however, has been produced to show that when of old Jeremiah challenged the character of being pre-eminent in misery, saying, "Behold, and see if there be any sorrow like unto my sorrow!" the friends of Christ may claim the pre-eminence for their Master; and, further, boast that when the prophet gave expression only to lamentations, their Saviour resignedly said, Thy will, O Father, be done! The apostle Paul, a comparison of whose case with that of Christ induced this long illustration, notwithstanding his heavy trials and eminence in fortitude, contemplates with admiration the example of our Lord; and draws from the manner in which He endured affliction one of the most consolatory lessons of our faith.

This Descant draws near its close. In its course so many subjects have been introduced, though not foreign to that originally proposed for illustration, yet slenderly connected with it in proportion to the space which has been given them, that some may have nearly lost sight of the main proposition. I therefore recall it to remembrance. It was the Honouring of God as a Father; and I conclude with an important and greatly-needed practical application of the discussion.

The Filial Honouring of God is pervaded, we have seen, in all its acts and manifestations by a joyful confidence in his Love. Now, there are many who, in place of this, offer us, in evidence of their being regenerated, a certain state of pleasedness of mind with CHRIST. There are few subjects which require to be more carefully scrutinised than this does. It is not *wholly* slander when the Socinian makes the charge against our evangelical profession, that it robs the Eternal Father of his glory. It is an undeniable fact that this system is in many instances so perverted, both in its preaching and entertainment, as to produce the alleged result. When with as much zeal as any, and more than the most, I denounce the Socinian, as having *no Saviour* in his creed, I equally denounce many of the self-esteemed orthodox as having *no Father* in theirs, but only something they call a Judge, looming darkly, far back in the distance. I know well enough that they speak at times of a Father in a systematic way; but the doctrine of a loving, warm Paternity is a stranger at once to the teaching of many and the experience of a great multitude, who endeavour to compensate for the want by speaking zealously for Christ, and, I question not, feeling towards Him a sort of warm affection. Let it be distinctly noted, then, that that is not the faith of the Gospel, the love and confidence of which *terminate* either *on* or *with* Christ. It is idle, and impertinent to the subject, to reply that Christ is God. Most devoutly I believe He is; but He is not the Father. And as Mediator (the principal, though not the only character in which we are called to contemplate Him), his work is to bring us back and introduce us, and reconcile us to the Father. So that, unless we "have received the spirit of *Adoption,* whereby we cry "Abba, Father," (Rom. viii. 15), it is not *that* Mediator's work which has been accomplished in us, but the work of some counterfeit of Him. Yea, Christian faith properly commences with persuasions of the Father's love in his essential paternal character; and from the beginning to the end of its course contemplates Christ as

M

being His Gift; so that the more it sees of Christ's preciousness, the more does it discover of the love of the Father, who gave Him. "In this was manifested the love of God toward us, because that God sent his only-begotten Son into the world, that we might live through Him. Herein is love, not that we loved God, but that He loved us, and sent His Son to be the propitiation for our sins." (1 John iv. 9, 10.)

APPENDIX.

(A)

TESTIMONIES TO THE DOCTRINE OF THE REWARD OF THE GOOD WORKS OF THE SAINTS.

SECTION FIRST.

TESTIMONIES OF CONFESSIONS OF CHURCHES OF THE REFORMATION.

I AM indebted for the contents of this section, the length of Calvin's Catechism, to the valuable work on Faith, of Dr. O'Brien, Bishop of Ossory.—I transcribe, with slight abbreviation and translation of the Latin occurring, Note Y, "Upon the Gospel Doctrine of Rewards."

"This doctrine is very distinctly laid down in the *Augsburg Confession*, Article VI. : "This *obedience*, therefore [of a believer] is accepted, not because it satisfies the Law, but because his *person* is in Christ reconciled by Faith. It is therefore always to be remembered that we obtain remission of sins, and that our *person* is pronounced *just*, i.e., *accepted*, gratis, for Christ's sake, through Faith : That after this, however, *obedience* to the Law is accepted also, and accounted righteousness in a certain sense, and merits rewards."—" The writers," says Dr. O'Brien, "repeat the assertion and caution most distinctly in the Article, On Good Works. They say, that the grounds on which our insufficient obedience is pleasing to God are necessary to be taught : "For it is not accepted for the reason that it satisfies the Law ; but because the *persons* of believers are reconciled and justified for Christ's sake, and believe that their imperfections are forgiven them.

Though, therefore, this new obedience is far from the perfection required by the Law, yet is it righteousness and merits rewards, for the reason that the *persons* are reconciled."*
——The same doctrine is taught in the *Saxon Confession*, Art. IX., How new obedience is accepted; and Art. X., On Rewards.——And among the Articles agreed upon by both sides at the *Conference at Altenburg* this was one: " That Good Works receive rewards both in the present life and in eternity."

The foregoing are the testimonies adduced by Dr. O'Brien from the Protestant Churches of Germany. He adduces the following from the Reformed Church of Helvetia or Switzerland, of which Zuingle was the founder, and Calvin a member; the latter of whom had probably a chief hand in drawing up the Confession.

Helvetic Confession, Article XVI.—"Those works which we perform through faith please God, and are approved of by Him: Because those *persons* are accepted of God, through faith in Christ, who perform the good works; which, moreover, are performed through the Holy Spirit, by the grace of God. . . . . For we teach that God confers a great reward on the performers of good works. This reward, however, we ascribe not to the *merits* of man receiving it, but to the *grace* or bounty and truth of God promising and bestowing it: Who, though He owes nothing to any one, yet has promised that He will reward His faithful worshippers; meantime

---

* Though Calvin approves of what is intentionally signified, yet he justly censures this mode of expression, in common use though it was with the Fathers. "What necessity," says he, "was there for the introduction of the word *merit*, when the value of good works might be expressed without offence by another term?" He does not give us one. I propose *qualification*. It *preaches* very conveniently: Qualify yourselves with rich qualifications of piety and charity for a large reward in heaven.

giving them even *that* wherewith they may worship Him. There are indeed many things dishonouring of God, and very many imperfect, to be found in the works even of the saints; but because God receives into favour, and embraces for Christ's sake the *persons* of the workers, He pays them the promised reward [to the extent, say the Westminster Divines of what is *sincere* in the work]."

Dr. O'Brien proceeds—"But I believe there is no opposition of views among the early Protestant divines upon this point." At least, he meets among writers of Reformation-renown only with Tyndale, who did not indeed deny that God has promised a reward, but censured the entertaining of the prospect as a motive to obedience, under the charge that it betrayed a mercenary, or as Primate French proclaims it, a hireling spirit! But why wonder at the *craze* of Tyndale (I now express my own sentiments) when the philosophic Edwards was similarly affected—verily *crazed*. I am persuaded, however, that the pious martyr knew not what manner of spirit he was of, and that it was much better than he imagined, in respect of honouring God by being actuated in his well-doing by the promise, as God designed he should be. In his answer to the base apostate, More *of Eutopia*, he says: "If I worke for a worldly purpose I get no rewarde in heaven; even so, if I worke for heaven, or a hyer place in heaven, I get, then, no rewarde: But I must do my worke for the love of my neighbour, because he is my brother, and the price of Christes blood, and because Christ hath deserved it, and desireth it of me, *and then my reward is great in heaven.*" Now, to represent a man as being thus persuaded of the reversion of a heavenly reward for all his work, and yet in the course of that work, toilsome and perilous as Tyndale's was, suppressing all thoughts of the reward as an encouragement to perseverance;

and only, after the work is done, comforting himself with that prospect—to make such a representation, I say, is the fancying of a monstrosity. Underneath his pietistic theory there must have been a heart alive to that influence of the divine promise, sustaining him amid privations and dangers, and inducing and impelling him onward in his holy enterprise. Only, I am persuaded that the prospect of reward was for him only a subordinate and secondary motive. It is this distinction of which Dr. O'Brien generously takes advantage in defence of the principles of one of the noblest spirits which shine in the martyrology of Protestantism. He pleads for Tyndale, that in the forequoted sentences his testimony against making the promise of reward a motive of obedience is directed only against making it the principal or primary motive. I doubt this. Calvin and Turretin, as will presently be shown, are earnest in calling attention to the distinction. But I fear that Tyndale expressed himself *absolutely*, as Jonathan Edwards did. It is the less to be regretted, when in the cases of them both we have good reason for believing that the soft, warm heart, sensitive to the divine promise, underlay the hard ice of the superficial intellectual theory—the pietistic *craze*.

CALVIN'S CATECHISM.

I adduce this Catechism under the first Section of Testimonies; for not only does it contain Calvin's individual opinions, but it was constituted a *symbolical* book of the Church of Geneva,—of the whole Reformed Church of France,—and, I note, specially, of the Church of Scotland. Probably it was the first printed and circulated system of Protestant faith in our country. At all events it was formally and authoritatively "approved" in the First Book of Discipline (Chap. xi. sect. 3), and usually printed with the Book of

Common Order.—With the exception of the word "impurity" being substituted for one less graceful at Ans. 122, I print *literatim* from Dunlop's copy, who printed from an edition of the year 1660.

121, *Minister.* Well, then, after that God hath once received us unto his favour [through justifying faith] be not the works which wee doe, by the vertue of his Spirit, acceptable unto Him? *Child.* Yes, verely; because He doeth of his free goodness so accept them; and not because their worthinesse doeth deserve so to be esteemed.

122, *Minister.* How is it that they be not worthy of themselves to bee accepted, since they proceede of the Holy Ghost? *Child.* Because there is mixed some impurity, through the infirmity of the flesh, whereby they are defiled.

123, *Minister.* By what means, then, are they made acceptable to God? *Child.* By faith alone; whereby a man is assured in his conscience, that God will not straitly examine his workes, nor trie them by the sharpe rigour of his justice; but that He will hide the imperfectnesse, and the unclean spots that be in them, with the pureness of our Saviour Christ, and so account them as perfect.

124, *Minister.* May we say, then, that a Christian is justified by his works [a second time] after that God hath called him, or that he doeth merite through them God's favour to the procurement of life everlasting? *Child.* No, verely; but rather it is said, that no man living shall be justified: and, therefore, we must pray that Hee do not enter into judgment with us. (Psa. cxliii. 2.)

125, *Minister.* Thou meanest not hereby that the good deeds of the faithful are unprofitable? *Child.* I meane nothing lesse; for God promiseth to rewarde them largely, both in this world and in the life to come: and yet, this notwithstanding, those rewards of God be not given for our worthy desertes, but only as it pleased God of his goodnesse to love us freely, and so to cover and forget our faults, that Hee will never call them any more to remembrance. [Good and clever *child*, that! Out of his mouth the Lord ordained great strength for the stilling of Antichrist in Scotland.]

THE REFORMED CHURCH OF FRANCE.

It has been stated before that Calvin's Catechism was adopted as one of the symbolical books of this once illustrious church, before it was overwhelmed by a deluge of blood on St. Bartholomew's day, to the exulting gratification of Archbishop Manning's Infallible Moloch. I am assured by a note of *Pictet* that their Confession bears good witness on the present subject.

THE PRELATIC CHURCH OF ENGLAND.

From this church, so far as its formularies are concerned, comes only a whisper. Primate Trench says of the term Reward, "that being a scriptural term, there is no reason why we should shrink from using it; as we find our church uses it in one of its Collects and in the Baptismal Service." I have discovered two other Collects which contain the idea. That's all for the transmitted Apostolicity!

SECTION SECOND.

INDIVIDUAL TESTIMONIES OF THE OLDER THEOLOGIANS.

CALVIN'S INSTITUTES.

"THE Institutes of the Christian Religion" was first published in the year 1536, about six years after the presentation of the Augsburg Confession. Calvin does indeed adopt and plead the principle of that Confession, that the *person* of the believer being accepted, his *works* become acceptable too; but his favourite plea is that a recovered believer's works being performed in the strength of the Spirit, in rewarding them the Lord only honours his own gifts. The Helvetic Confession, as we have seen, drawn up to a great extent under Calvin's influence if not chiefly by his own hand, combines the two principles; and it is a fault in the Westminster Confession that it does not do the same, and especially with such a good exemplar before them.—I have felt great difficulty in making a selection of the testimonies which abound in chapters xv., xvi., xvii., and xviii., of Book III. of the Institutes. I hope the specimens I furnish will induce brethren in the ministry to dig for themselves in the golden mine.

Chap. xv. Sec. 3.—"The good works which the Lord has conferred on us [by his Spirit] He denominates our own; and declares He will not only *accept* but also *reward* them.—It is our duty to be animated by so great a promise; and to stir up our minds that we be not weary in well-doing; and to be truly grateful for so great an instance of divine goodness."

Chap. xv. Sec. 3.—"Good works are pleasing to God, and not unprofitable to the authors of them; and they will moreover receive the most ample blessings from God as their reward, not because they *merit* them, but because the divine goodness has freely appointed them this reward."

Chap. xv. Sec. 4.—"The doctrine of the Scripture is that our good works are perpetually defiled by many blemishes.— Yet, because in his great mercy God does not examine them according to the rigour of his justice, He *accepts* them, as though they were immaculate and pure; and therefore *rewards* them, though void of all merit, with infinite blessings, both in this life and that which is to come [*i.e.* according to the Westminster Divines, 'that which is sincere' in them]."

Chap. xv. Sec. 4.—" Whatever is now conferred on the faithful to promote their salvation, as well as their future blessedness, flows exclusively from the beneficence of God. Nevertheless, He declares, that both in the latter and the former He hath respect to our works; because to demonstrate the greatness of his love to us He dignifies with such honour not only ourselves [our persons] but the gifts [our works] which He hath bestowed on us."

Chap. xv. Sec. 2.—" God is equally liberal in assigning a reward to good works, as an ability to perform them."

Chap. xvi. Sec. 3.—" Nor do I say this [having exposed the Popish doctrine of *merit*] because I either reject or neglect that kind of exhortation, which the Scripture frequently uses, that no method of animating us to our duty may be omitted. It mentions the Reward which God will render to every man according to his works.—But that this is the only argument, or the principal one, I deny. In the next place, I confess that we ought not to begin with it." [The primary arguments are explained, with great force and beauty to be respect to the glory of God and a sense of duty. See extract from Turretin.]

The Seventeenth Chapter of the Third Book of the Institutes is titled, The Harmony between the Promises of the Law and those of the Gospel.—I might say that the argument is most *ingenious*, if such commendation would not, in the reckoning of some, detract from its character for *solidity*.—I earnestly recommend the study of the whole of the Chapter, especially to ministerial brethren, as opening up a clear way for their employment of the *legal promises* of the Old Testament, in the comforting and animating in well-doing of saints under the New Testament. Calvin goes back to Sinai, lays hold on those promises, in the name of Christ, and triumphantly transfers them to Zion.—The following extracts are all of which my space admits. But though they may convey imperfectly an idea of his argument, yet they will establish beyond dispute that point for which I at present more especially contend, viz.: That that great Reformer, after whose name, as the arch-hierophant of their faith, so many surreptitiously denominate themselves, not only admitted, but strenuously contended for, *that* which they in their pretentious concern for the purity of the doctrines of Free Grace revile as a heresy—even that doctrine, that God is not unrighteous to forget the work and labour of love of his children, but will remunerate them with a great recompence—This was Calvin's opinion, and he thought, in his simplicity, the arrangement was eminently one of grace.—I proceed with the extracts.

Chap. xvii. Sec. 3.—"What then? it will be said. Were those promises [of the Law] given to vanish away without producing any effect? I have already declared that this is not my opinion. I assert, indeed, that they have no efficacy with respect to us, so long as they are referred to the *merit* of works; wherefore, considered in themselves, they are in some sense abolished. (Rom. x. 5, &c.) But when these are superseded by the promises of the Gospel, which proclaim the gratuitous remission of sins, the consequence is, that not only our *persons* but *works* also are accepted by God; and not accepted only, but followed by those blessings which were due by the covenant to the observance of the Law. I grant, therefore, that the works of the faithful are rewarded by those things which the Lord has promised in his Law to the followers of righteousness and holiness."

Chap. xvii. Sec. 8.—"Now we describe this [personal] righteousness in the following manner:—That a sinner being admitted to communion with Christ [united to Him], is by his grace reconciled to God; while being purified by His blood he obtains remission of sins; and being clothed with His righteousness as if it were his own, he stands secure before the heavenly tribunal. When remission of sins has been *previously* received the good works which *succeed* are estimated far beyond their intrinsic value; for all their imperfections are covered by the perfection of Christ, and all their blemishes are removed by His purity, that they may not be scrutinised by the divine judgment. The *guilt*, therefore, of all transgressions by which men are prevented from offering anything acceptable to God being obliterated [at justification], and the [subsequent] imperfection which universally deforms even the good works of the faithful being *buried in oblivion*, their works are accounted righteous, or, which is the same thing, are imputed for righteousness.

Chap. xviii. Sec. 6.—" Make to yourselves friends of the mammon of unrighteousness [deceptive riches]; that, when ye fail, they [the authorities] may receive you into everlasting habitations." (Luke xvi. 9.) "Charge them that are rich in this world, that they be not high-minded, nor trust in uncertain riches, but in the living God; that they do good; that they be rich in good works; laying up in store for themselves a good foundation against the time to come, that they may lay hold on eternal life." (1 Tim. vi. 17-19.) We shall never arrive, he says, at the true meaning of these passages, unless we advert to the design of the Spirit in such language. If Christ's declaration be true, that "where our treasure is there will our heart be also," as the children of this world are generally intent on the acquisition of those things which conduce to the comfort of the present life, so it ought to be the concern of the faithful, after being taught that this life will ere long vanish as a dream, to *transmit* these things which they really wish to enjoy to that place where they shall possess a perfect and permanent life. It behoves us, therefore, to imitate the conduct of those who determine to migrate to any new situation where they have chosen to reside during the remainder of their lives. They send their property before them, without regarding the inconvenience of a temporary absence from it, esteeming their happiness the greater in proportion to the wealth which they possess in the place which they intend for their permanent residence. If we believe Heaven to be our country, it is better for us to transmit our wealth thither than to retain it here, where we may lose it by a sudden removal. But how shall we transmit it? Why, if we communicate to the necessities of the poor, whatever is bestowed on them the Lord considers as given to Himself, to be repaid, according to the promise. (Prov. xix. 17.) And again it is promised, " He which soweth bountifully shall reap also bountifully." (2 Cor. ix. 6.) For all things that are bestowed on our brethren in the way of charity are so many deposits in the hand of the Lord, which He, as a faithful Depositary, will one day restore with ample interest. Are our acts of duty, then, it will be asked, so valuable in the sight of the Lord, that they are like riches reserved in his hand for us? *Who can be afraid to assert this*, when the Scriptures so frequently and plainly declare it? But if any one from the mere *grace* of God would infer the *merit* of works, these testimonies will afford no countenance to such an error. For we can infer nothing from them except the indulgence which God in his mercy is disposed to show us, since, in order to animate us to rectitude of conduct, though the duties we perform are unworthy the least notice from Him (?), yet He suffers not one of them to go unrewarded.

TURRETIN'S INSTITUTION.

One great advantage of Turretin's Elenchical, *i.e.* error-refutative, Theology, is that he came after Bellarmin. — Bellarmin coming after Luther, Zuingle and Calvin and their reforming coadjutors, had with his confessedly great powers perfected in his Disputations the Popish argument. Nothing had theretofore appeared equal, and nothing has appeared since superior, or even of much consequence as supplementary. All the forces of Popery having been thus arrayed b his skilful generalship, when Turretin with his Protestant array demolishes — truly *demolishes*—them, the theological student may save himself the trouble of doing anything more than clothing himself out of the armoury of the Elenchics of Turretin, *Contra Pontificios*. Thus armed *cap-a-pie* he is prepared for any encounter with the foe.— The following is not a very favourable specimen of Turretin's powers—the argument is so easy as to afford little opportunity for their display. Besides, though I have translated as well as I can, there is a precision in the logical expression of the original which I have failed to communicate.—I note that the passages of scripture quoted in Sect. 13 do not occur in the Elenchics; but are transferred from one of his Disputations where the same *relations*, &c., are repeated.

· Division (*locus*) xvii. Quest. v. Sects. 12, 13, 14.—*State of the question on good works.*

Sec. 12. "The Question is not (1), If good works please God and are accepted by Him, and obtain from Him a reward of [eternal] life: For we admit this willingly to our opponents, provided the reward be understood to be one of grace and not of debt. (2) The question is not, If it be lawful to work with the prospect of a reward: For we doubt not that this may be done, a two-fold caution being observed;

first, that the prospect of a reward be as of one of gratuitous *præmium*, and not of equitable *price;* and secondly, that [as an animation to work] it be not looked at alone, or principally and primarily, but subordinately and secondarily, after the glory of God, which is here before all other ends to be kept in view by us."

Sec. 13. (3) "The question is not, If works have any *relation* to eternal life ; and if there be established any fitness *(convenientia)* and proportion between good works and eternal life : For we admit that there is established a relation of *order and connection* such as subsists between means and an end (Jo. iii. 5, Luke xiii. 3, Matth. v. 8), a way and a goal (Ephes. ii. 10, Phil. iii. 14), a conflict and a crown (1 Tim. vi. 12, 2 Tim. ii. 3, 5), an antecedent and a consequent ; and that there is constituted a *fitness and proportion* such as obtain between things of the same order— as between sowing and reaping (Gal. vi. 7, 8), first fruits and main crop (Rom. viii. 22), the commencement of anything and its completion. [All this is granted.] But the question is, If good works bear to eternal life the relation of a *cause,* properly so called ; and if there be established betwixt them a proportion of equality and commensurateness [Calvin calls it *reciprocalness*]. This we deny."

Sec. 14. (4) "The question is not, If God be bound by *covenant* to recompense good works with a reward : For we do not deny that since He has given a promise He is necessarily engaged to fulfil it; and that He has thus, in a certain way, become a debtor, not to us, but to Himself and His own Faithfulness : But the question is, If works from their intrinsic value and worthiness merit and obtain the reward promised by God, and in virtue of which they can be properly said to *effect* salvation : Our opponents affirm this ; we deny it."

How lamentable, yea, how strange, it is, that all this excellence of distinction should be marred by that "fly in the ointment" at Ques. 2nd, where an *excuse*, as it were, is made for any saint who may be found deriving any animation in well-doing from God's promise of a reward! Calvin, as we have seen, on the contrary says it is *dutiful* to do so; and Dr. Lawson, as we shall afterwards see, says it is *sinful* not to do it. But let this pass.—Turretin having stated his propositions, proceeds to their illustration and proof. There is no need for following him: for besides that the statements with the distinctions carry proof in themselves my object at present is chiefly to adduce this theologian of renown as one who gives his testimony to the doctrine of the Saints' Reward—a purpose which has been already served.—An additional observation, however, will be useful.—The difference of the degrees of reward, according to the difference of the degrees of faithfulness, is implied in all the distinctions which he makes; and I think declared expressly in his use of the phrase, "fitness and *proportion*," in Sect. 13. But there can be no doubt of his views being expressed strictly in Sect. 42, as follows:

"Though different degrees of glory be ordained, so that God should remunerate graciously the peculiar labours and sufferings of the pious with peculiar rewards, both temporal and heavenly, yet nothing can be thence concluded in favour of the *Aureolæ;* because not only glory in general, but all the degrees of it are plainly gifts of grace."

The *Aureolæ* are golden crowns of peculiar splendour which the Popish Doctors teach will be bestowed, according to the promises, Rev. xiv. 4, Daniel xii. 3, Rev. ii. 17, made respectively to Virgins, Doctors, and Martyrs, and which the painters represent by the *nimbi* encircling their heads.—

Now, though Turretin is right when he censures the Doctors for their ascribing the preference to *merits*, and also right when he censures them for limiting the promises to the *three literal* parties, yet he errs, and acts inconsistently with himself, when he mocks as he does in Sect. 40 at their general idea of the Aureolæ. It is as scriptural as it is beautiful. (Rev. iv. 4.) I am persuaded that Turretin himself will be glorified with an aureola of peculiar brightness.—The explanation, I suspect and fear both from this and what was previously noted, is that Turretin's *sentiments* were not favourable to the doctrine of diversity of degrees of glory; and that a scriptural scholarship and logic *enforced* it on his judgment. So much the worse for Turretin's *sentiments*, but so much the better for the *doctrine*, as evincing the compelling strength of evidence in its favour.

MACCOVIUS'S COMMON PLACES.—AN. 1640.

Chap. lxxiii.—On the charge of Mercenariness.

Here a question occurs: Is it lawful for the pious to do good in prospect of a Reward? There are some who say that this is abhorrent to the nature of a saint, but they appear to me, *first*, to divest man of human nature; *secondly*, to censure God, who so acts towards man as to propose a reward to him; and, *thirdly*, to condemn the holiest of men who have acted in expectation of a reward. They say that it looks base and unworthy of a son, that he serve his father either in hope of a reward or in fear of punishment, and that this is to act the part of a mercenary. I reply, that reward and punishment may be regarded in two different ways. *First*, absolutely of themselves; and, *secondly*, as they are images and representations by which the goodness and severity of the invisible God are signified to us. Now the difference betwixt a mercenary and a son is this, that the mercenary regards the reward and punishment *absolutely*—has respect to nothing in them but the reward and punishment themselves; whereas the son contemplates in the one his father's goodness, and in the other his anger. But nothing more becomes a son than that he dread incurring his father's displeasure, and that he indulge himself in the contemplation of his goodness.

WITSIUS'S ECONOMY.—AN. 1693.

Book III., Chap. xiv., Sects. 39 and 40. On the diversity of the heavenly felicity and glory of the saints.

"Here it is usual to inquire, whether there will be any difference of degrees among the blessed. In this question, though we utterly disclaim the proud doctrine of the Romanists concerning the disparity of glory founded on the inequality of *merits*, yet the arguments of those who think that God will crown the inequal measure of the *gifts of grace* with a disparity of the *gifts of glory*, seem more probable to us. To this purpose are these Scriptures, Rom. ii. 6, and 2 Cor. v. 10; by which is not barely signified the quality of the free reward which shall be granted the righteous, according to their works; but also the quantity of that reward, answering in a certain proportion to their works. This is expressly explained by the Apostle, 2 Cor. ix. 6, 'He which soweth sparingly,' &c. Moreover, that this harvest and its diversity, or different product, is erroneously confined to this life, appears from comparing this place with Gal. vi. 8. To the same effect is 1 Cor. iii. 8, where it is clearly declared that the proportion of the reward will be adjusted to that of the labour. Nor unlike to this is the discourse concerning the resurrection of the dead (1 Cor. xv. 40, 41); where first the bodies laid aside at death are compared with those assumed at the resurrection; and, *besides*, the celestial bodies are said to differ very much in glory from each other. And to what purpose is that distinct mention of sun, moon, and stars, and of the inequal glory of each, if the Apostle only intended to teach us the difference of the terrestrial from the celestial bodies, if all the celestial were to have the same glory?"—[I consider this to be *demonstrative*, in answer to the slighting manner in which Dr. Dick treats its evidence, in a passage not altogether worthy of him, and which Dr. Wardlaw censures. A special reason for this remark will appear afterwards under another testimony.]

In Sect. 40th, Witsius exposes the opinions of those who cannot but admit that special honour is assigned in the Scripture to certain individuals and certain classes, but who contend that the distinction is only for this world, or will be made merely by *commendation* pronounced on them in the day of judgment.—Of the promise made to the Apostles, Matthew xix. 28, he says. "To confine this glory to the Apostles within the limits of the church militant in such a manner that in the triumphant they shall quit their thrones, seems repugnant to reason: nor does it agree with John's vision, who saw in heaven four-and-twenty thrones, and four-and-twenty elders sitting on them, and having on their heads crowns of gold (Rev. iv. 4)." And of the "commendation," he argues, that since it is to be inequally distributed, in proportion to diligence and success, it is presumptive evidence that there shall be inequality in other distributions also.

These testimonies of older theologians have already received their full proportion of space in these pages, and a number must be withholden which were collected from the writings of Pictet, and others of eminence; all of the same tenor with those which have been recorded.

SECTION THIRD.

TESTIMONIES OF MODERN THEOLOGIANS.

When we leave the rich pastures of the two preceding sections and enter this, what a barren wilderness, comparatively, it is! So that my illustrations, instead of being consistent with the title of the section, will assume the appearance of being rather evidence against the doctrine for which I contend; those in reputation for piety and learning who bear witness for it being so few, and some of the few giving their evidence so partially (in part only) and so coldly. I begin with those whose Lectures, as Professors of Theology to the various evangelical denominations, have been published. Think then of this, that notwithstanding the manner in which the Scripture is replenished with the encouragement of the promise—the testimonies to it of all the churches of the Reformation as given in their confessions, the Church of England alone excepted—the testimony of the Westminster Assembly, composed of the elite of Episcopalians, Presbyterians, and Independents—the testimonies of Calvin, Turretin, and all the Calvinistic fathers and their sons for more than a century afterwards—think, I say, that notwithstanding all this the following should be the state of matters now:

(1.) *Dwight's Theology.*—Throughout the five volumes 8vo, the idea of a saint being rewarded for his own works does not once occur.

(2.) *Dick's Theology.*—In Lecture lxxii., in answer to the objection that the doctrine of Justification by Faith is injurious to the cause of good morality, one of the replies, as made in about half a page, is to this effect: that the doctrine encourages obedience, inasmuch as it assures believers of that of which others cannot be assured, that, as justified in Christ, they "work under the eye of an approving witness and *gracious rewarder*." This is well put; but it is all that the four 8vo volumes contain favourable to a doctrine which bulks so largely in the Volume of our Hopes. Besides, the little that is good is neutralised, when in Lecture lxxxiii. it is said, "Whether there will be different degrees of glory in heaven is a question more curious than useful;" and which the subsequent few remarks show rather an inclination to negative.

(3.) *Hill's Lectures on Divinity.*—In Book v. chap. iv. sec. 2, we meet with the following sentences: "Protestants hold, that although the good works commanded in Scripture, and produced by the influence of the Spirit, give the person who maintains them a real excellence of character by which he is superior to others—by which he is 'acceptable to God and approved of by men,' and in respect of which he is styled in the Scriptures 'worthy,'—yet, they do not constitute *a right to claim* anything from God as a reward;—that the expression frequent in Scriptures, 'God will render to every man according to his deeds,' implies that good works are a preparation for heaven, or an indispensable qualification for the promised reward; *And* that there will be a *proportion* betwixt the virtuous exertion here and the *measure* of the reward conferred hereafter; but that good works are not in any respect the procuring cause of the Reward; for the reward is represented as 'of grace, not of debt,' flowing from the promise of God upon account of the merits of his Son."—Here again, I remark, as in the case of Dr. Dick's morsel, the case is *well put* in opposition to the Popish doctrine of *merit;* but equally, I exclaim, when it is all that occurs in the three volumes 8vo, How inadequate it is to the magnitude of the subject as contained in the Divine System of Theology! in which, I maintain, the Reward of Grace for the saints' own works bulks as largely in form (Grace forbid, I should say, as importantly!) as the Reward of Merit does for Christ's work. It would appear that but for the antagonism to Popery this Reward of Grace would have been passed by unnoticed by many of our Systematic Doctors, leaving a multitude of texts of Scripture without a key of interpretation; and in their dealing with which hundreds of the weaker brethren blunder and flounder in their lectures and sermons so pitiably, having no guidance from their Masters.

(4.) *Chalmers's Institutes of Theology* (2 vols., 8vo, 1849).—It is impossible to give, within the narrow compass which these sheets allow, an adequate account of the contents of the three chapters (viii., ix., and x.), which bear on the subject now immediately before us. And I must content myself with an indication of a few prominent points. No one who knows anything of the eminent preacher and divine can doubt that his Systematic Discussions will be Scripturally sound and leal to Protestantism, in witnessing for the doctrine of Justification by Faith alone in the Atoning work of the Redeemer. But few will be prepared—I who in my youth followed him every where, was not—for the bitter scorn with which he denounces and exposes in these lectures the self-called and popularly reputed evangelicalism of the present day; on account of its faithlessness in the proclamation and inculcation of the necessity of Good Works, in conjunction with Justifying Faith. I thought I had gone far enough in the exposure of " the Zealots," as I have called them. But mine is suavity and gentleness compared with his onslaught. Not only does he go further than courtesy permitted me to go, but further than I can follow him in a spirit of justice. *My* complaint is of a want of inculcating good works on the ground, though a subordinate one, of a promised reward; *his* complaint is of a want of their being inculcated on any ground whatever, and of our evangelicalism having degenerated into a virtuousless antinomianism. Nor is it in measured terms he makes the accusation, "Let your works be," he says, "not those of penance and mortification, but works of righteousness and charity, and then shall your light break forth as the morning. The Reformers have demolished the former works, and made noble demonstration of their vanity; but we fear that as the controversy thickened, a withering influence has been cast on *all works*, and men have looked hard at them, as having at best an ambiguous and questionable place in Christianity. There is all the difference in the world between the free, fearless, urgent, and unqualified manner in which the apostles press home the observance of them, and the feeble, tremulous, hesitating testimony in their favour given by many of our modern evangelicals, who beset their every exhortation to practice with so many cautions and adjustments, we could almost say apologies, that it falls with uncertain sound upon the hearer—so that, instead of abounding in the work of the Lord, because knowing that his labour is not in vain, he, as if lost in the mists of an artificial theology [elsewhere called "the freezing influences of an ill-understood orthodoxy"] is bereft of all confidence and all comfort in the way of obedience." (Vol. ii., p. 281.) In page 282 he thus expresses himself, "We affirm it to be a great *desideratum* that this grand constituent of a living and personal and real Christianity (inclusive both of acts and principles) should be re-instated, should be restored to the place which it undoubtedly has in the Scriptures of the Old and New Testaments; but which it has not in the popular mind of

Christendom." And in page 279 he speaks of it as a great "distemper" of the church, requiring the remedy of an earnest inculcation of Good Works, that there is a very numerous class, he fears, " who have come under the delusion that, somehow or other, faith without works is to save them; and so look askance at the preacher who tells them that they must cease to do evil and learn to do well. Instead of which they like a great deal better if he just keep harping on the phrases of a cabalistic orthodoxy, which is altogether in word, and not at all in power." He, therefore, at page 285, calls on the theological students under his training to " Go forth in the battle against this Hydra of Antinomianism, that subtle and deep-seated delusion which operates so extensively, we fear, throughout the popular mind in all Christian lands. Enter on an unsparing warfare against it."

There is a great deal more in the same strain. To use his own expression, he *harps* on the charge. I have already signified that I do not concur with him to the extent of his censure ; but the more was I led to anticipate that he would instruct his young warriors to use as one of their weapons for slaying the hydra the proclamation of the doctrine that the good works of the saints are rewardable and will be rewarded, —when lo ! he turns round and fulminates his censure against it even with more fiery indignation if possible, than he had done against antinomianism. He does not indeed attack the doctrine specifically and by name. With all his bravery he could not well exhibit to scorn and reprobation that grand distinction with which alone the Fathers of the Reformation, and the Westminster Divines to boot, found they could meet the misinterpretations of the Popish Doctors—the distinction, viz.: of Rewards of Debt and Rewards of Grace. The Doctor could not but know it ; but he makes no sign that he did, and in contempt of it launches forth in invectives against the *principle;* stigmatising as "mercenariness," and "sordid hireling selfishness," and "marketing for heaven," should a man be influenced in his conduct by a respect to his own interests. He far transcends Madame Guyon and Edwards, whose *pietism* was directed especially against *the loving of God* for his benefits. Chalmers contends that *all morality whatever* is vitiated if there enter into the motivity any regard to self; and if virtue be not pursued quite disinterestedly for the sake of its own loveliness. "You will perceive," he says at page 224, "the infinitely higher character of that morality which is loved and cultivated for itself, over that morality which is rendered at the bidding of another and for the sake of a something distinct from itself. By this change in its object it in fact ceases to be morality, and assumes one or other of the forms of selfishness." [What then comes of working or being self-denied at the Divine *bidding?*] Again, he says at page 225, that the conception that "virtue is the hard and revolting labour that must be submitted to, in return for an equivalent, distinct from the virtue that earns it,"—that "this conception is greatly fostered by those elements of a right and a claim and a legal challenge to reward, which are all bound up in the dispensation of—Do this and live;"— that "this marketing for heaven belongs to the very essence of legality; and it is impossible to compute how much morality is vulgarised by it."—There is much more to the same effect: and is it not a strange way of speaking of *that* "Do this and live," which was the divine legislation for Adam in innocence? But this is not the place for refuting this irrational, unnatural, and anti-scriptural *craze,* and under the aberration of which he becomes at times so self-contradictory. I have already in the text, at page 83, to which I refer, answered the objection made, under the charge of Mercenariness, to our being animated in the discharge of duty by the divine promise of a reward: and I dismiss these Institutes with painfully disappointed feelings, that I have not gained the name of their venerated author as a witness for a truth of such moment.

(5.) *Cunningham's Historical Theology* (2 vols).—In these volumes, highly worthy of a student's consultation, we meet with only a few sentences, and these very general and vague, which have any bearing on our present subject. (Vol. ii., p. 108.) Had the historian lived to *fill up* his Lectures, he could not have failed to give a more special account of the manner in which the Reformers met, by means of the doctrine of the *Reward of Grace*, the misinterpretations of those many passages of Scripture from which the Popish doctors deduced their dogma of the *merit* of good works. The question engages a large portion of Calvin's Institutes, and is importantly historical.

(6.) *Wardlaw's Systematic Theology* (3 vols).—In the review of theological systems we have at last lighted on what is consistent with the title of the section—a satisfactory testimony. Nothing can be more explicit and less hesitating than the manner in which this great master in scriptural dialectics pronounces in favour of the doctrine of diversity of degrees in the blessedness and glory of the saints. He sees no difficulty in the subject. Not only does he regard the scriptural evidence clear and express, but he argues that the distinguishing of some above others is *required* for the manifestation of the divine character. "It is evidently necessary," says he (vol. iii., p. 712), "that in every department of his administration the blessed God should manifest, not only his delight in mercy, but *his love to righteousness*. (Psa. xi. 7.) Now, in the final judgment there are two ways in which we may consider this part of his character as displayed. *First*, in the great general ground on which all the blessedness of heaven shall for ever be bestowed on each individually, and the countless millions of the redeemed, namely, the all-perfect mediatorial righteousness of Immanuel. . . . The *second* way in which God will manifest his character will be, by the characters of those whom He will then accept, and by the *proportioning* of the honour and joy bestowed to the degree in which that character had been sustained. . . . It seems to me that this idea of proportion is implied in the simile used by the apostle of the correspondence of the harvest to the seed time; for we have the image both as it respects the kind of seed sown and the quantity. (Gal. vi. 7, 9; 2 Cor. ix. 6; 1 Cor. iii. 6, 8.)" In the section next to that from which I have just quoted (at page 714), when Christ says, "if any man serve me, him will my Father honour," our author asks and appeals to our moral sense: " Does He mean? —Can He mean, that He will honour all who serve Him alike, whether that service has been vigorous or feeble— ardent or cool—zealous, persevering and efficient, or comparatively slack, inconstant and unproductive?" "*It cannot be*," answers the moralist. And to a similar subsequent question he answers again, "It cannot be."

I had noted much more for quotation, but my limited space affords room additionally only for his conclusion, in answer to such as may admit that a reward is promised, but object to our being influenced in well-doing by the prospect of it; for that there may be such the case of Tyndale is an evidence. "It is very evident," he says, " that the very principle of proportion which we have been endeavouring to place on a scriptural basis ought to operate as an incitement to the exercise of a self-denying and self-devoting zeal. There is surely such a thing as a legitimate ambition in this service, a holy emulation of activity—faithful persevering activity in it—with an eye to the recompense of reward. Is not the parable of the Talents *intended* to encourage, by teaching the lesson that it is required 'according to what a man hath, and not according to what he hath not?' And is not the parable of the Pounds *intended* to animate to emulous exertion by teaching another lesson, that the honour will be according to the measure of the diligent improvement and corresponding results of the same means: ten cities to the servant whose pound yielded a return of ten pounds, and five to him who could report only five pounds? When Peter exhorts Christians to diligence, he adds: 'For if ye do these things ye shall never fall: for so an entrance shall be ministered unto you abundantly unto the everlasting kingdom of our Lord and Saviour Jesus Christ.' (2 Peter i. 10, 11.) What means he here by the word 'abundantly?' There is surely some difference between an entrance and an abundant entrance." (pp. 717, 718). And he proceeds to illustrate the case by the contrast of two vessels entering port, the one gallantly and richly laden, the other all damaged in equipment and cargo. But surely our author has failed of his usual accuracy of illustration. It is not the ship and its cargo with which the idea of abundance is connected, but the *entrance ministered*—ministered by the owner of the ship, or the Lord of the country when He abundantly rewards the faithful crew. Robert Hall, as we shall presently see, states the contrast as lying betwixt those who have an "abundant entrance," and those who are "saved as by fire;" and Mr. Binney expands the statement into a magnificent oration. But my present object is to display testimonies to the Reward of Grace, without examining strictly the sufficiency of the arguments by which the witness-bearers reach their conclusions. And I dismiss Wardlaw's volumes with a kind of triumph that I have found in them a testimony so clear and decided by one whose name stands second to no other in the list of modern theologians since the day of Turretin. Were I to say that it stands *first* for logical acumen and force, both analytic and synthetic, together with devout respect to the Scripture, what is the name which any one, who may mock at my judgment, would give us as its equal? *Quandoque bonus dormitat Homerus;* and lamentably did Wardlaw sleep on the subject of the Coming of the Bridegroom; but this is characteristic even of the *wise Virgins* (not of Chalmers, though, in his last and holiest days); and it does not hinder those who are awake to acknowledge their indebtedness to the sleeper for the manner in which he did assist them, and though dead still speaking does assist them to replenish their vessels with oil.

(7.) *Russell's Letters* (2 vols).—Though these letters do not rank formally with those Professorial *systems* which have been reviewed, yet I adduce their evidence here because Letters xii. and xiii. contain matter more pondered by a highly-qualified mind than any with which I have met in my search for testimonies. Besides, I feel a certain gratification in giving juxta-position to the sentiments of Dr. Wardlaw and of Dr. Russell, who as denominational brethren walked together in such harmony, and co-operated so zealously for the Faith.—Notwithstanding, however, the manner in which I have expressed my opinion of the excellence of Dr. Russell's contribution to the present argument, it is impossible to give a satisfactory account of it in my limited space. As being contained in Epistolary Correspondence, though by no means desultory it consists principally of special observations, without any strict method being observed of logical and consecutive discussion. The most of these observations, more or less extended, may be classed under the following topics: First, that it is clearly a Scriptural doctrine that there shall be a diversity of felicity and glory among the saints in heaven, according to the diversity of character and well-doing on earth.— Second, that the pre-eminence of the higher class shall not have *merit* for its cause, but follow by necessary moral sequence, or be conferred by a special act of the *grace* of God.—Third, that the diversity of felicity will partly proceed from the different degrees of susceptibility of enjoying heavenly scenes and exercises—that susceptibility being according to the culture of the mind in this preparatory state.—Fourth, that the diversity of honour and glory will partly proceed from the different degrees of capability for station, that capability being according to the acquirements made in this world. The church in heaven, as well as the church on earth, will be an organised society, the more important functions and higher offices being by the necessity of good administration conferred on those who are best qualified to *lead* in the exercises and work of the kingdom, whatever they may be (vol. ii., p. 202.)—Fifth, that in addition to these two necessary sequences there will be a declaration and manifestation of the peculiar personal delight of God in those who have in this world been peculiarly faithful.—Sixth, that by the prospect of higher delight from increased susceptibility—of higher honour from increased capability for station—but especially of higher approbation of God and closer communion with Him, we should be animated more and more in all our heavenward preparation, whether of work or sentiment.

These and some other points are stated and illustrated briefly or more at length, with Scriptural confirmation and impressive reflections. I leave these Letters with expressing my persuasion that, as the discussion of this subject proceeds, they will, when reprinted, work as efficiently for the popularising of the doctrine of the Reward of Grace, as the venerated author's Treatise on the Salvation of all who die in Infancy has done, for the overthrow, now nearly accomplished, of a dogma by which our faith was so dishonoured, and the minds of the weak were so burdened with horror.

TESTIMONIES OF THE SECESSION CHURCH OF SCOTLAND.

Few will complain, I think, that it is in this section of the Church especially I search for evangelical testimonies, so far as Scotland is concerned, for nearly a century prior to the time of the present generation. And yet I am of the opinion expressed by Dr. Merle D'Aubigné, when speaking of Moderatism, that neither before that secession, nor since, has the State-church been chargeable, to any considerable extent, with opposing or even ignoring the doctrine of Salvation through faith in the Mediatorial and Atoning work of Christ, or with a *legalism* which inculcated good works, as meritorious of heavenly felicity.* Confessional and Catechetical Doctrine was always preached widely. Not only would the people, deadened though they were, yet with the Catechism universally in their memories, and the New Testament universally in their hands, not have tolerated anything to the contrary; but it was much easier for the

---

* I find, on re-reading Dr. Merle's *Luttes en Ecosse*, that he refers rather to the state of Moderatism as it preceded the last Disruption, the first which was spiritually by far the more important, having ameliorated matters. But I allow the statement of the text to remain as expressive of my own opinion.

weak and slothful then, as it is for such characters now, to preach orthodoxly, than to indite "such moral essays as the heathen Cicero might have written," for which Moderatism vulgarly but so absurdly *receives credit*. What a pity it is that those orations *De officiis* of Scotch moderate divines have not come down to us! Moral Essays! explaining and enforcing, of course on Christian principles, Truthfulness, Honesty, Candour, Meekness, Liberality, Sobriety, Chastity, &c., and denouncing Falsehood, Fraud, Slander, Envy and Pride, Selfishness, Drunkenness, Sensuality, &c., why, such moral essaying is, according to Dr. Chalmers, the grand *desideratum* of the present day, and the want of it the great *distemper* of which the church needs to be cured. But such essay-writing requires more time and labour than many can spare, and more wisdom, discrimination, and fortitude, too, than many possess; and it is a great deal more convenient to string on the thread of some catechetical common-place (the *requireds* and *forbiddens* of the commandments always excepted) a few Heads and Particulars, like the Paternosters for the one and the Ave Marias for the other, of an old popish wife's Rosary. Such orthodoxy abounded among the Moderates; and the grand evil was the *moderation*—the drowsy, perfunctory, get me-over, haste-me-done, soulless, lifeless manner, devoid of earnestness and zeal, in which sound doctrine was mouthed over. To awaken the church and nation out of this Laodicean torpor was the special mission of the Secession Fathers : the vindication of Christ's rights over his own house, without interference by king, patrons, or judges, and of the people's rights to elect their own ministers, being only a subordinate and comparatively rude, though important, part of their testimony and work.

In the execution of their commission they gave the Mediatory office of Christ, as Prophet, Priest, and King of the Church, its proportionate place, as the fundamental, central, all-pervading principle of the system—a proportion which Moderatism, with its formal orthodoxy, did not allow it. Of this extensive magnifying of Christ, for the contemplation and "receiving" of Faith, the enemy took occasion to accuse them of overlooking or undervaluing or disparaging the personal righteousness of His people. How false the accusation! Though it may have been partly with the view of repelling this charge, yet, irrespectively of it—from jealousy of the Divine honour—jealousy of the character of the doctrine of Justification by Faith—jealousy of the honour of their church-fellowship, there was never a class of men, throughout the history of the church, by whom good works were inculcated with greater earnestness and urgency, and, which is of great consequence, spirit-trying particularity. Seceders and Moderates, as teachers and inculcators of morality, not to speak of personal exemplifiers of it! It is a burlesque to compare them.

Ebenezer and Ralph Erskines! *Par quam nobile fratrum!* We must go back to the time of the Apostles ere we find the like of it for a combination of natural and spiritual brotherhood; and even then Peter and Andrew, and James and John will not furnish adequate types; neither, though we go further back, will Moses and Aaron. We must look on high to the *Gemini* of the starry heavens for a fitting symbol. Well, from the two quarto volumes of Sermons by Ebenezer, and the ten octavo volumes by Ralph, from which, as spoken and printed, Seceder-preaching got its *cast* or *set*, I am prepared to furnish a system of Ethics as pure elevated and comprehensive, inculcated with as much earnestness, in proper portion, on the Practice of the saints, as of a system of Christology of glory and mercy, displayed for the reception of their Faith.

Their moral teaching proceeded in the following manner: First, *Negatively*, or rather, in the order of *Contrariety*. With the view of shutting up their hearers to Faith on the Atonement and merits of Christ, they excelled the Moderates in their faithful exposures of the natural depravity of the heart, and dispelling delusions of any works possibly proceeding from it which could gain salvation. It is a first principle in the teaching of Virtue and cultivating the moral sense, to expose the odiousness and worthlessness of Vice. Some moralists and preachers do little more. It is easier. The Secession Fathers did as much as any and more than most in this way; but they did not stop here, they proceeded—

Secondly, *Exhibitively*. In portraying, as they delighted to do, the spotless innocence of the Lamb of God as a fit sacrifice for sin, they indirectly cultivated the moral sense of the beholders. According to the next distinction, they employed this holiness of Christ directly as an authoritative example; but even when they were employing it merely in illustration of the value of his sacrifice, the exhibition of the picture of venerableness and loveliness was powerful for moral impression.

Thirdly, *Derivatively*. With the salvation of the Cross as the ground of their plea for a life of holy and virtuous obedience on the part of believers, they appealed to their sense of Gratitude to God as the bestower of the mercy—to their sense of Justice towards Christ as having purchased them by his blood, so as to bind them to the obedience of his law and the following of his example—and to their sense of the necessity to prepare themselves with holy habits for the holy inheritance which by his cross He had secured for them. Some other motives to obedience they derived from the same source; but let the statement of these as the principal for the time suffice.—Dr. Chalmers himself was once accustomed to preach the Derivative *process* with great fervour. But, in his latter days, in his Institutes, after stating the argument with much fairness, though he does not entirely give it up, yet he treats it as being of so little consequence as virtually to discard it, and insists on the Commandment being preached *in its own right*, independently of motives to its obedience being derived from the Redemption of the Cross. (Vol. II. pp. 207-209.) Under what motive then?—the Sovereign *bidding* of God? Not at all; for then the conduct "ceases to be morality, and assumes one or other of the forms of selfishness." What then? "The excellence of virtue in itself," he answers! (Vol. II. p. 224.) Such transcendentalism had no place in the ethics of Seceder-theology; unless their preaching be considered to partake of that character, when in subordination to the *derivative* argument, they would at times recommend a holy virtuousness for the venerable, exemplary, and useful character with which it clothes the saint, and the peace of conscience with which it blesses him.

Fourthly, *Evidentially*. Their mode of reasoning with their people was this: Saving Faith in Christ necessarily produces Good works. If therefore on an examination of your conduct the good works are not discoverable, you may be certain that you are not possessed of the faith, but only some counterfeit of it, and have need to begin at the beginning and acquire it. On the other hand, if on a wide—not partial—review of feelings and conduct you find a *good* measure of righteousness—as much as *characterises* your life, though there are remains of evil,—dismiss your suspicions of the genuineness of your faith, and go forward joyfully to perfection.—Is there any faithful minister of the Gospel who goes through a Sabbath's services, without having plied his people more or less urgently with this evidential argument? Dr. Chalmers plied it powerfully in those days, when he produced a revival, if I should not call it a revolution, far more glorious than the comparatively rude Disruption. And yet, in his Institutes, there is nothing which he treats more scornfully. "We hold," says he, "that virtue has been degraded to a secondary rank by a vast number, perhaps by the majority, of those writers who are termed evangelical. It is so degraded when represented merely as the Evidence of Faith. We are not sure that in one view they have not made a farther remove from the real importance of virtue and the honour which is due to it, than even the legalists. They make virtue but the index of Faith; and so reversing the apostolic maxim that Charity is greater than Faith, they would make Faith greater than Charity—that which is indicated being greater than that which indicates. . . . With them it is neither the money nor the money's worth. If I may use so strange a figure, it is but the reflexion of that money in a looking-glass." (Vol. II. p. 229.) This is as unjust as it is bitter—as scornworthy as scornful.

Who may be the multitude of writers whose works the satirist had fallen in with I know not; but this I know that the Secession Fathers, with the illustration of whose preaching I am presently engaged, never represented charity, or any other virtue, as being *merely* the Evidence of Faith. I admit, however, yea, boast of it—that they *did* represent Faith in the once crucified and now glorified Christ as being *the* cardinal virtue of New Testament morality. They did not speak of it by that name, as neither did they, of Charity; but it is as much of a virtuous character as Charity is. They called both *graces*, as being gifts of God; and Christian ethics have not profited by the culture (!) which has changed the nomenclature. But let that pass. They *did* magnify the grace of Faith above that of Charity, inasmuch as *through* it a sinner is saved from endless woe and constituted an heir of immortal bliss—pardoned and adopted—a state or condition to which no Charity, howsoever liberal and disinterested, could ever introduce or advance him, but only enrich his enjoyment of it. No man ever enforced this in his preaching, nor can enforce it as he does in these very Institutes, with greater ardour than Chalmers himself. And yet, under the spell of his *craze* about disinterested virtue, he turns round on Faith, and taking advantage of the apostle's representation of its being only a temporary grace for this dark world, degrades it, with all its *salvation-power*, below Charity which has no such power; and which is superior only in the quality of permanence, when its parent Faith has been transformed in the Beatification of Vision. Using his own expression about others, I repeat he *degrades* Faith by equalising it with any other virtue; whereas it is the mother of all the virtues; yea, by treating it as if it were no virtue at all: But I forget: " Believe and thou shalt be saved" (Acts xvi. 31) contains an appeal to *self-interest*, every whit as strong as " Do this and live;" any acting according to which we have already seen he condemns as essentially *immoral;* though it was divinely promulgated the law for Paradise.

I proceed with the illustration of the scriptural wisdom of the Seceders.—In their pleadings for Faith, as the one Great

Virtue, through which salvation is communicated by divine holiness and mercy, they did indeed, and I celebrate them as sensible men for having done so, earnestly and strictly demand of their hearers the exhibition of Charity and all the other virtues as an *index* of the genuineness of their profession of that Faith—as being a necessary *outcome* from it; and the want of which convicted the profession of hypocrisy or self-delusion; so that the pretenders needed to commence anew and "lay foundations."—But they did not *merely* and always plead the cause of good works in this *posterior* way. They frequently commenced with illustrating the excellence and necessity of Charity, and then came to the question, How is such a virtuous frame of mind to be acquired? Well, what answer did they give? Was it, that their people should study, and contemplate its moral beauty, till charmed with the loveliness they should embrace it for its own sake? The imagination of a Seceder doing so is ludicrous. They referred their hearers to the Cross, by the believing contemplation of which they knew this Charity would be generated and fostered. They had a sharp eye those old Seceders, for both "money and money's worth," and could not be imposed upon by any "reflexion of that money in a looking glass" of virtue indulged in for its own sake. They demanded the bright and solid gold; and knew that Faith was the only mint for the precious coinage. They imitated Paul as a financier in raising funds. When he needed money for the poor saints in Jerusalem, his plea with the wealthy Corinthians was, "Ye know the grace of our Lord Jesus Christ, that though He was rich, yet for your sakes He became poor, that ye through his poverty might be rich." (2 Cor. viii. 9.)

How sorry I feel, yea how chagrined, that I must stop short

in my enconium of that noble Seceder-Ancestry, and take up my parable against them! So far as that special subject is concerned, for testimonies to which I am in quest, I must consign the Erskines and their Sermons over to the company of Chalmers and his Institutes. I have ransacked the two quarto, *plus* the ten octavo volumes, without finding one sentence favourable to the doctrine that in the distribution of heavenly rewards the saints shall be distinguished from one another according to the different degrees of their faithfulness. Nay, the use of the term "reward" is carefully eschewed, except in a few instances in which it is applied to the heavenly inheritance in general, succeeding *in course* the Christian pilgrimage, as when the storm-beat traveller when he has reached the warmth and cheer of home might say he was well *rewarded* for the pains of his journey. There is a sermon of Ebenezer Erskine, on Titus iii. 8, which was justly very famous in its day, and had great power in influencing evangelical preaching, not only in the Secession but throughout Scotland. It is titled, "The Necessity and Profitableness of Good Works Asserted." Well, at the very point where logically, and systematically, according to Calvin and the Westminster divines, the Rewardableness of Good Works should have been introduced, illustrated, and displayed for encouragement, the flow of eloquence is arrested, and the oracle becomes dumb.—Reason 7th is thus stated: "There is an analogy and *proportion* between good works and glory." Some might suppose that the term "proportion" used here, implied *differential* rewards. But it is afterward explained as signifying merely "an aptitude and meetness for partaking of the inheritance of the saints in light," there being "a connection of congruity and suitableness between begun holiness here, and consummate holiness hereafter."

I feel as if I had done an injury to the memory of an eminent saint and divine, when, for greater convenience of illustration, I have referred to the two Erskines, without noticing a *spiritual* brother, who, though not by his preaching, yet, by his pen, did as efficient service as any of them for promoting the grand Spiritual Disruption. Let me now redeem the wrong. Fisher's Catechism! It is a principal glory of the Faith, the Mental Philosophy, and the Theology of Scotland. In scholastic subtlety of distinction it equals that of Aquinas and Scotus, when it is clothed with a charm of piety, and advances with a power of scriptural proof in which they were so deficient (only, he was greatly indebted to their logic and made good eclectic use of it;) and nothing so strongly convicts the present generation—not to speak of inferior piety—of mental imbecility, compared with that of the preceding, than the manner in which that book once so popular is now so little appreciated. I must explain to the ignorant what is its nature. It is a system of theology on the basis of the Westminster Shorter Catechism (12mo, pp. 520.) Ebenezer and Ralph Erskines assisted Fisher in composing and revising the first half, and it was published (1753) with the sanction of Ebenezer, Ralph having died shortly before. Ebenezer died soon after, so that the authorship of the second part, and responsibility for its contents belonged entirely to Fisher; though he assures us that it was submitted to the inspection of several of his brethren before publication, so that it appeared as a *quasi* Testimony of the whole of the Secession church. —But notwithstanding my expressed admiration of Fisher, I must, as in the case of the Erskines, sorrowfully indite a *palinode*.

On the subject of the Reward of the good works of the saints the following is all that occurs. It lies at Questions

52 and 53, under Question xxxviii. of the Shorter Catechism, on Benefits received at the Resurrection, of which one is "the full enjoying of God."

Question 52. In what respect will the communication of God [in the beatific vision] to the *experience* of the saints in heaven be *full?*—A. Inasmuch as they will not be stinted to any measure; but the enjoyments will go as far as their most enlarged *capacities* can reach. Q. 53. Will the capacities of the saints above be of *equal size?*—A. As there will be *different degrees* of glory, (the saints in heaven being compared to stars which are of different magnitudes, Dan. xii. 3), so some capacities will contain more, and others less, yet all shall be filled and have what they can hold.

This is something; but, at best, it is little to be all. And yet, it is equivocal; for the question is not answered, Whence the difference of capacities? And in other parts of his book Fisher appears to deny by his silence that the previous good works have any effect in enlarging the capacity, at least in the way of gaining it as a reward. Had he been sufficiently impressed with this he could not well have avoided expressing it in the two following instances: (1st), At Qs. 37-39 under Q. xxvi., on Christ as a King, giving laws to his people, he thus proceeds: Q. 37. Doth He annex any *rewards* to the obedience of his true subjects?—A. Yes: In keeping of his commandments there is great reward (Ps. xix. 11). Q. 38. What are these rewards?—A. His special comforts and *love tokens* which He bestows for exciting to that holy and tender walk which is a fruit of faith. Q. 39. Why are these *comforts* called *rewards?*—A. Because they are given to a working saint as a further privilege on the back of duty.—That's all of the Royal Reward of Christ, by which, as a key, the whole of that large body of New Testament promise to obedience is to be opened for encouragement !—How lamentable it is that good men, under the power of a perverse or defective system, will tempt us to mock at that which is true and holy, when, although but part of an answer (sometimes not even that, but pertaining to some other subject,) they propose it as the whole of the truth, and sufficient for an inquirer !— (2nd,) Our Catechist repeats the omission when under Ques. xxxv., on Sanctification, he at his own question, No. 45, asks and answers thus: Q. For what good *end* and *use* is Sanctification necessary?—A. Not for justification before God, but for evidencing our justification and faith. It is necessary for glorifying God and showing forth his praise; for adorning the doctrine of *God our Saviour;* for proving our union to Christ; for promoting inward peace and rejoicing; for maintaining fellowship and communion with God; for making us meet for heaven, because without holiness no man shall see God; for making us useful to men on earth; for stopping the mouth of calumny when we are reproached as evil doers.—This is just a summary of a great part of the famous sermon of Ebenezer Erskine to which I formerly referred—ending where he ended, so unsatisfactorily and so far short of the Testimony of the Scripture, which so expressly, so emphatically, so abundantly sets forth the prospect of being rewarded with a peculiarly high degree of glory in heaven, as a motive for cultivating a peculiarly high degree of grace in this world.

How shall we account for this glaring defect in the teaching of those eminently pious and learned men? It could not proceed from their being ignorant of the grand distinction of the Reward of Debt and the Reward of Grace, which was one of the principal weapons with which the Reformers fought their battle, and with which the Westminster Divines stored their armoury for the combat whether with Papists, Legalists, or Antinomians :—Neither could it proceed from their feeling that there was a large portion of the Scripture which they could interpret satisfactorily without its aid:— Nor could it proceed from the fear of being reported by zealots as *unsound*, for at that time the zealotry lay with the Moderates, whom the use and pleading of Reward in any form would have propitiated rather than incensed; and when our recent zealotry was only being generated by their own default. Besides, they were not the men to be deterred by fear of human censure from proclaiming what they regarded salutary truth. The only explanation which remains is, that though they believed the doctrine—had subscribed it as comprehended in the Confession—yet feared that, in the circumstances, their teaching of it might be so misinterpreted by the people as to mar their belief in the doctrine of Justification by Faith alone, which they valued more highly than that of the Reward of Grace. How insufficient and groundless this apology was I have shown when remonstrating with brethren of the present day who make the same defence of their mutilating the gospel. (p. 42.)

But whatever may be the right explanation of the defect of the Secession Fathers, its maimedness was transmitted extensively to their sons, not only of their own ecclesiastical denomination, but throughout the evangelicalism of Scotland in the established and all the dissenting churches. These twelve volumes of Sermons and Fisher's Catechism, published in tens of thousands of copies, were universally Text Books. The recent Disruption was Erskinite not only in similarity of principle but through *transmission* of principle; and its members are of a more thorough breed than the *nominal* Erskine family are; for the latter have *grown out* of what they regard a deformity, in views of earthly establishments of the faith, by which the Erskines were disfigured, whereas the former retain it. But whatever may be thought or said of this, it is undeniable that *almost the whole* of their progeny, of whatever name, have retained their *halt* in eschewing the preaching of the doctrine of the differential Reward of Grace. I do not say *universally.* The testimony which I am about to produce is not only of itself an exception; but the mode in which it is expressed, having nothing polemical in it, and being chiefly exhortative, indicates that the doctrine was not novel or strange: so that probably there were both preaching and printing on the subject which I have neither heard of nor seen. But they cannot have been extensive. I have made considerable research, and found no clear and decided utterance in its favour till more than sixty years after the death of the last of the Erskines. That testimony however on which I have lighted, as given at that time, is of great price, not only on account of its intrinsic excellence, but the venerable character and high position of its author.

LAWSON'S SERMONS.

Dr. George Lawson, of Selkirk, was Professor of Divinity to the Associate Synod (1786-1820), which in union with the Synod of Relief, formed what is now the United Presbyterian Church of Scotland. Rarely has any teacher been so venerated by his pupils. I extract from a volume published in 1818, two years before his death.

"It will not be necessary at present to explain the consistency of the reward given to the Labourers in the Vineyard (Matt. xx.) with the freeness of that Grace by which eternal life is bestowed on us as the gift of God, through Christ Jesus our Lord. Our only plea of *admission* into heaven must be 'the righteousness of God' by faith: for by the works of the law shall no flesh be justified. ☞ But it ought to be remembered that if our *persons* are accepted in the Beloved, our *works* also are accepted; and although they cannot *go before* us to heaven, to open the gates for our reception, they *follow us*, that we may lose none of those things which we have wrought, but may receive a full reward" (p. 241).

" If you are in Christ, your works are accepted for His sake; and if God is pleased with them, He will crown them with testimonies of his approbation. Nor will it be evidence, either of a mercenary or of a self-righteous spirit, to look for that acceptance, and those rewards which are assured to you, by exceeding great and precious promises. You do not suppose that Moses was a man of a self-righteous or mercenary spirit, and yet 'he had respect unto the recompense of the reward.' You must certainly pour contempt both on the authority and grace of God, if you disregard at once his commandments and promises, by refusing to look forward to his promised [reward of] grace to animate your diligence in his service. Does not Paul enjoin you to be 'steadfast, unmovable, always abounding in the work of the Lord, forasmuch as ye know that your labour shall not be in vain in the Lord?' Does not Jesus say, 'When thou makest a feast, call the poor, the maimed, the lame, the blind: and thou shalt be blessed, for they cannot recompense thee: for thou shalt be recompensed at the resurrection of the just.' You will doubtless act under the dominion of a self-righteous spirit, if you hope to be *justified*, either wholly or in part, by your own works. But if you believe in Christ for justification, you ought also to trust Him for the acceptance of your good works: not that they are to be associated with his own works, as the foundation of your hope in God, but that they are to be richly and graciously rewarded, through the Beloved, according to his promise. Were we not [first] justified freely by the grace of God we could not reasonably hope that any of our works will be accepted. One sin is more than sufficient to overbalance all our good works. But if our sins are entirely purged away [in justification], and we are enabled [afterward] to perform works truly good, however imperfect, they must be well-pleasing to God, through our gracious Intercessor " (p. 215).

"It is plain that in the parables of the Talents and the Pound (Matt. xxv. 29; Luke xix. 17-19), there is an intimation of a difference to be made amongst the blessed in the heavenly rewards. But it would not appear to be the intention of our Lord to teach this doctrine, however certain and important, in the parable before us (Matt. xx., according to which all the labourers are equally rewarded), which was designed to repress the vain glory ready to spring up in the minds of Christians who enjoy some advantages above others, and to excite those who labour under disadvantages to be the followers of those who are before them in the Christian course. Although there is a diversity of the rewards in heaven, they are not measured by the length of time in which persons have laboured on earth in the service of Christ. Many have been sincere Christians in the past part of their life whose attainments have not equalled those of other Christians who have spent a considerable part of their lives in the service of iniquity " (p. 242).

Some may question the venerable Doctor's explanation of the design of the Parable. But that will not affect his testimony to the doctrine of the *diversity* of the saints' rewards, which he regards as being "certain," from other Scriptural proofs, and which he does not in the least found on this parable, but rather treats it as being at first sight contradictory of that which is a favourite doctrine with him, and from which he endeavours to defend it. Be his interpretation in this instance right or wrong, we are sure of his having entertained as a principal article of Christian faith, that the good works of the saints shall be rewarded, and proportionally to their excellence; and moreover, that instead of stigmatising it as being legalist, and mercenary and hireling, and violatory of the doctrine of Free Grace to entertain the prospect, he denounces it as being certainly a pouring of contempt both on the authority and grace of God, if you disregard at once his commandments and promises by refusing to look forward to his promised gracious reward to animate your diligence in his service.

My jubilation over this testimony is short-lived. Though it occurs in a popular sermon, it indicates such warmth of feeling for the subject, that it cannot but have engaged a part of his professorial prelections, but my search for fruits among his pupils has been almost vain. Without limiting my observations, however, to the preaching of those who enjoyed the training of that Master in Israel, and taking the widest scope, I remark—

(1st.) These sixty years—the term of my capability of understanding sermons—I have never heard one—and I have heard many by ministers of all denominations—in which the doctrine of the Reward of Grace, in proportion to faithfulness in Good Works, was preached for the rebuke of the slothful and the encouragement of the diligent—*excepting one*, about fifty-two years ago, by the late Dr. Thomson, the leader of the evangelical party in the Established Church. I have good reason to remember it, when, being yet a student of theology, it fixed a principle for me,—that though a saint's works are not the *meritorious cause* of heavenly glory, yet they are the *measure* of it. " Enlarge your measures, therefore," was the appeal of the eloquent preacher.—(2d.) I have inquired at a great number of aged christians of various denominations, without finding one who remembered that he or she had ever heard a sermon in which Good Works were recommended on the principle of their being distinctively and proportionally rewarded.—(3d.) Although among my ministerial brethren and acquaintance of various denominations I have met in private with only one who opposed the doctrine, yet I have not discovered so many as ten who told me that even once (in the course of long ministries in some cases) they had preached the doctrine, or uttered the word Reward in the pulpit, except in condemning the heresy of *meritorious* Reward; or when in routine they read the Scriptures, or prescribed the Nineteenth Psalm as matter of praise : their apology being the old one, that they feared, were they to preach the Scriptural doctrine in its entireness, the people might pervert it through misapprehension to *legalist* ends.

Again : Excepting the Systems of Theology already noticed, I have not discovered anything printed and published on the subject since the days of Dr. Lawson, excepting what is noticed as follows :

(1st.) A passage of the late *Dr. John Brown*, Edinburgh, on the heavenly reward of faithful office-bearers, in his commentary on 1st Peter v. 4. But the remarks, though in their place excellent, are limited in respect both of the persons rewarded, and the nature of the reward; and do not contain any statement of fundamental principles.—(2d.) Two expository observations by the late *Dr. Lindsay*, Professor of Exegetical Theology, in his Lectures on the Epistle to the Hebrews: the first at chap. vi. 10, the other at chap. x. 35. Both are clear and decided. I quote from the second: "Heaven is the glorious inheritance that awaits the people of God. This blessedness is procured by the work of Christ, but it is bestowed as the Reward of Faith. It is not a reward earned by us, so that we can claim it as a debt; it is altogether of grace; but still its *distribution* is regulated according to the attainments of believers: just as a father may bestow gifts upon his children to which, strictly speaking, they may have no claim, and still may *proportion* his favours to the assiduity and diligence of the different members of the family." —(3d.) A testimony by Dr. N. M'Michael, Professor of Church History to the United Presbyterian Church; whose Lectures by their various qualities of excellence, are at present of such advantage to his pupils, and which, in course of time (*longum absit dies!*) will, when published, be of such advantage to the church at large. In a paper which appeared in the *Christian Journal*, January, 1845, he thus expressed himself:—" How many even of God's children—we will not speak of mere professors—would be confounded and offended with a bold and *intelligible* statement of the doctrine of Rewards, under the Christian economy! Ignorance, indolence, the re-action of Popery have all tended to throw this subject into the background: but the times demand that it be brought out from the dust and rubbish of centuries, and held up to the view of the church till its beauty and importance be recognized by all."—Such a critical note, however, in a Magazine is comparatively of small importance. From the commencement of his ministry Dr. M'Michael has systematically preached the doctrine of the Reward by Grace of a believer's own works, as a complement of the doctrine

P

of Justification by Faith in the work of the Redeemer.—(4th.) An observation by *Dr. John Eadie*, Professor of Exegetical Theology to the United Presbyterian Church. It occurs in his Exegesis of the Epistle to the Ephesians, in high repute even with the scholarly divines of Germany. At chap. vi. 9, he annotates thus:—" The Christian doctrine of Rewards is too often lost sight of, or kept in abeyance, as if it were not perfectly consistent with the freest [most gratuitous] bestowment of heavenly glory."—Well, I appeal to my learned friend, that he take advantage of the honours he has gained for Scriptural *lore*, and help us, poor scholars, in turning the misdirected eyes of the church to this precious truth, and in having it redeemed from the abeyance, *i. e.*, imprisonment, in which it is kept; and more especially when his gifts as a rhetorician cope with his accomplishments as a scholar, in rare combination.—(5th.) A passage in a sermon of the late *Rev. J. Hay*, United Presbyterian minister at Arbroath, of good repute as a scholar and divine. The sermon is titled, The Trials and Rewards of the Missionary, and was published in the *United Secession Magazine*, February, 1836. Among other matters of similar import he expresses himself thus: "God entices and encourages his people by the promise of a glorious recompense, as in the words of our text. (Mark x. 29, 30.) The principle of a holy ambition to acquire the Rewards of Grace is not incompatible with the supreme love to God, which is the reigning motive to all obedience in believers; otherwise the Redeemer had not appealed to it here. Nor has the promise of a glorious recompense to his faithful disciple any inconsistency with the doctrine of salvation by Free Grace, to the exclusion of all merit; for the Reward is wholly gracious, not meritorious; and indeed the attraction of it can be felt by none but those who are already partakers of salvation by grace."—(6th.) A passage in a volume of Sermons, all of rare excellence, by the late *Rev. Alexander Jack*, United Presbyterian minister at Dunbar. In the passage to which I specially refer (Sermon xi., The Final Assize), and for extracting which I am sorry I want space, after running a well-pointed contrast betwixt inferior, or "ordinary believers," as my next witness-bearer calls them, and those of a superior class—for earnestness and self-denying labours of piety and benevolence —he appeals with irresistible force, if it do not shock the moral sense to represent them as being at last equalised in glory. The distinction betwixt the reward of merit and the reward of grace, receives from him, of course, its due acknowledgment. —(7th.) A paper by the *Rev. Dr. Andrew Sommerville*, which appeared in the Missionary Record of the United Presbyterian Church, for March 1862, titled, The glory that awaits those who are instrumental in converting sinners. He commences with a graphic description of the heavens in a starry night, and then proceeds thus—"It is this scene of surpassing loveliness and grandeur which the Divine Spirit has chosen as the emblem of that glory which awaits those who are the means of winning souls to Christ. 'And they that be wise shall shine as the brightness of the firmament; and they that turn many to righteousness as the stars for ever and ever.' (Dan. xii. 3.) Ordinary believers—those who are wise in spiritual things, but who have done little for the salvation of others, shall shine as the brightness of the Firmament; whereas those who have been very zealous for the Lord, and who laboured in turning sinners from the error of their ways, shall obtain far higher degrees of honour, and shall shine like Stars in the firmament for ever and ever. And the same thing may in measure be affirmed of those who from love to Christ and his gospel contribute of their substance for upholding and extending the interests of truth.—The Bible tells us that 'every man shall receive his *own* reward according to his *own* labour.' (1 Cor. iii. 8.) That reward, given in grace, will correspond to the work done for Christ. All who are saved in the Lord will be perfect, blessed, and glorious; but those who have been most faithful shall, in the exercise of God's rich beneficence, be rewarded with marks of superior commendation."—Toward the conclusion, having adverted to the circumstance, that in our foreign mission fields the stars shine out with a lustre and beauty never seen in our comparatively dim and moist atmosphere, the missionaries, he says, "have therefore nightly before their eyes a peculiarly radiant memorial and interpretation of the great promise to which we have referred. God says to them in times of sadness, 'Lift up your eyes on high, and behold Who hath created these things, that bringeth out their host by number: He calleth them all by names, by the greatness of his might, for that He is strong in power; not one faileth. He fainteth not, neither is weary. He giveth power to the faint; and to them that have no might He increaseth strength.' (Isaiah xl.) This is high consolation; but there is *more* than this to be seen and heard *there*. Just as God has placed his Bow in the cloud, in the day of rain, as the sign of his faithfulness, so, it may be said, He has woven the promise of future recompense with beams of light into these resplendent constellations; and that the voice which comes to them nightly is, Behold in those effulgent luminaries an image of your coming honours; and as 'one star differeth from another star in glory,' so will it be with the servants of God in the heavenly state. Wherefore labour on and weary not; abound in deeds of faith and love; and fixing your eyes on the brightest of these sparkling orbs, seek, by turning many sinners to righteousness, to gain the peerless distinction which it typifies amid the everlasting glories of the celestial world."—This is astronomy eloquently spiritualised. But we must make allowance for the favouritism with which everyone regards his own special calling. Dr. Sommerville, as secretary to a great Missionary Institution, and having charge, in the observatory, of the telescope, marked Daniel xii. 3, has cleared the glasses, and turned it toward the Castor star of Missions, and says, Come and see, how beautifully glorious! A brother astronomer who is specially engaged with that marked Matthew xxv. 35, 36, 40, having turned his towards the Pollux star of Charity, says, Come and see, how gloriously beautiful! Dr. Sommerville takes a look, and frankly admits the equality in splendour; and says to his brother, I will keep my lenses bright for the observation of Castor, keep yours bright for the observation of Pollux, and let us occasionally interchange services, that we may charm the people into the ambition of being similarly irradiated, by our display of the united glories of the whole Constellation in the highest heavens. Most heartily agreed, says Dr. Guthrie.

I close this department of my review, with a testimony which will make some compensation for the preceding meagerness. It is frequently told of Bishop Usher, as for his praise, that he said he was resolved to die, praying like the publican, " God be merciful to me a sinner!" I hope he died in a better mood. The publican's example was incongruous for one who by the grace of God was what Usher was.—He, whose memory I now celebrate, chose for his example the long-tried faithful Paul (2 Tim. iv.), rather than that of the publican just entering on the new life of holiness. The late *Dr. John Mitchell*, distinguished for his literature as the prize-taker for the essay on the evangelization of India, and eminent in position as a Professor of Theology—one in whom piety, wisdom, and meekness emulated one another for the praise of being his characteristic grace—in a pastoral letter addressed to his church from his sick chamber, where he waited for death, expresses himself thus:—" I say it with deep humility—I trust through the grace of our Lord Jesus Christ, bestowed on his servant, my record is on high; and my welcome and reward are also there—a reward the more glorious because entirely gratuitous."—There would be more among us—both ministers and people—of this happy Paul-like experience, were there more of its sound Pauline doctrine—a similar fidelity in work being precursory, in which I know a goodly number of brethren in all denominations to be well qualified. May divine Grace multiply their number, with similar expectations of their being *rewarded* for it all in the kingdom of God!

TESTIMONIES OF ENGLISH NON-CONFORMISTS.

I have not had either time or opportunity for exploring this field: nor as a Scottish Presbyterian do I feel so much interest in it as in that which I have just left; but I suspect from what I have found, or rather not found, that, though I had explored extensively, my findings would have been scanty. It will be observed that three of the witnesses whom I am about to produce speak of the doctrine as uncommon. Hamilton and Binney say so expressly, and when Hall says, that the inspired writers evince "no reluctance" to employ the term "reward," he evidently insinuates that his neighbours do, much the same as brethren in Scotland.

Robert Hall's Sermons. Notes by his own hand. No. xxxiii. On the Reward of the pious in Heaven.

"The felicity which awaits those who persevere through good and evil report in a stedfast adherence to Christ is expressed in scripture by the name of Reward. The inspired writers evince no reluctance to employ this term; but still we must never lose sight of its true nature—that it is "of grace and not of debt." It is what the infinite condescension of God is pleased to bestow on those who love Him; not what any man can claim as equitably due; not to say, that the ability to perform the works is the effect of renewing and sanctifying grace; so that, while in one sense they are *our deeds*, they are in another *his donations*.—The felicity which God will bestow on his faithful servants may be properly denominated a Reward on the following accounts: (1) It is inseparably joined to obedience; and is promised as a motive to encourage and sustain it. Christ will be "the author of eternal salvation to them," and them only, "who obey Him." (2) It will be bestowed expressly as a mark of approbation and acceptance of the obedience to which it is annexed. It will be bestowed as a token and demonstration of God's complacency in righteousness. (3) The reward—the felicity bestowed—will be *proportioned* to the degree of religious improvement—to the work of faith and labour of love. We are reminded of those who are "saved as by fire," and of those who have "an abundant entrance"—of a *righteous* man's, and of a *prophet's* reward—of some who "sow sparingly," and of others who "sow bountifully," both of whom shall reap accordingly."

The subsequent Notes are on the certainty, the satisfactoriness and eternal duration of the heavenly rewards, as contrasted with the character of those of this world. I doubt not that in preaching from his syllabus, the impressive rhetoric of Hall, in the second part of his discourse, excelled the illustrative theology in the first; yet the theology must have been interesting and valuable; and meeting in the desert with its indications, though it be but as a sprig of juniper tree, it is a refreshment to be seen and good spoil for my conservatory.

Dr. Richard Winter Hamilton's Congregational Lecture. (Twelfth Series, 1847), on the Revealed Doctrine of Rewards and Punishments. Eight Lectures: No. II., on the Harmony of Revelation with Natural Religion: No. III., on the Nature and Rewardableness of Christian Virtue.

It would require a volume of the size of the present to simplify for common intelligence the christianized Philosophy, or the philosophized Christianity of this remarkable work. But my object at present is not so much to place before my readers the arguments of my authorities, as simply to adduce them as witnesses to the truth for which I contend. And I might satisfy myself with the statement that Dr. Hamilton, one of the first scriptural critics and ethical philosophers of the age, and preferred by his non-conformist brethren to the highest honour they can bestow, not only warmly entertained the doctrine of the Good Works of the Saints being distinctively Rewarded, but treated the denial of it now with indignation and now with contempt. I will extract a passage, however, as a specimen, to induce brethren in the ministry, especially, to study the whole work :—

" We now enter upon an inquiry which passes beyond the fact and the doctrine of Reward: we investigate what may be called its philosophy. Are virtuous affections and acts, in the circumstances that we have supposed, rewardable ?—Can the contrary be imagined ? Could it be gravely urged ? Is it fitting, reasonable, agreeable to right, consonant to the nature of things, that they be considered and treated as proper subjects of Reward ?—Should we succeed in our proof, one thing may be demanded. We must be shamed out of constant apology for the term itself. We are bound as openly to declare the doctrine as any other. In maintaining all truth we shock many classes and orders of feelings: why are they [the zealots] who oppose the theology of Christian rewards only to be accommodated and soothed? Are they the most worthy defenders of divine grace? Are they the most devoted asserters of morality? Are they the men of large views, of connected ideas, of holiest principles? We must revere the diction of Scripture, and not refine upon it.—If it be objected that a *mercenary* feeling is implied in this idea and expectation, we disclaim once for all that religion ever proposes itself to an abstract disinterestedness in man. Such a tenet [as held by Madame Guyon, Edwards, Chalmers, Froude, &c.] holds not with the first speculative view of Law. It contradicts all the love of happiness and fear of misery, which are our earliest conscious emotions ; [it dehumanizes man, says Maccovius]. It is at variance with our probationary position during the present life. It wars with every sanction of obligation. The greatest exercise of reason, the best conduct of understanding to which we can have recourse, is to seek the most extensive measure and the most durable continuance of good. We are not called to 'serve God for nought' [Satan's pretentious transcendental ethics]. We are warranted to anticipate 'profit,' if we *pray* to Him. Every duty is but a path to the pleasant direction and cheerful use of our being. Every sacrifice is secured by its ample indemnity. Every restraint is the prevention of so much ill. A proper self-love finds in religion a perfect expatiation. It is a 'fulness of blessing.' This is reciprocally explained and understood. *God* [on his part] declares it: 'that they may fear Me for ever, for the good of them.' *His people* [on their part] avow it: 'Lord, to whom shall we go but unto Thee?

Thou hast the words of Eternal life.' We need not, then, apprehend that the purest sentiments of piety, the most disinterested repose on the divine beauty, the most complacential veneration and esteem, the warmest spontaneousness of gratitude, can in anywise be impaired by the creature's necessary desire and pursuit of happiness." (pp. 198, 199.) Page after page, to a great length, follows, containing similar, and, in some cases, superior matter. But with much regret I must dismiss the Book: only, I must subjoin the explanation, to meet the possible objection of the zealots, that the "circumstances supposed," to which Dr. Hamilton at the beginning of the extract refers, are the circumstances of a pardoned believer, received through faith into the family of God, by the atonement of Christ. No zealot can plead the doctrine of justification by faith alone more decidedly and earnestly; nor can any zealot, his mind being shown by his zealotry to be of an inferior stamp, plead it with such exactness of scriptural interpretation, and philosophical defence and exposition of it on the principles of Eternal Moral Law.

T. Binney's Sermons (1869) Sermon vii.: Salvation by Fire and Salvation in Fulness.

The preacher discourses from those two texts: 1 Cor. iii. 15. "If any man's work shall be burned he shall suffer loss; but he himself shall be saved; yet so as by fire:" and 2 Peter i. 10, 11, "If ye do these things ye shall never fail: for so an entrance shall be ministered to you abundantly into the everlasting kingdom of our Lord and Saviour Jesus Christ."

Robert Hall had previously, we have seen, contrasted those two texts. It is not likely that Binney knew of it, for it lies in an obscure portion of Hall's works. But it does not signify whether he knew of it or not. It is sufficient for my purpose that both of those eminent divines (see Wardlaw also on the "abundant entrance") have understood the texts as declaring differential degrees of glory in the world to come for saints of different degrees of grace in this. Possibly, Hall, with his great gift of Platonic and Howe-like contemplation, in preaching from his syllabus excelled Binney in illustrating the heavenly glory; but I feel certain that Binney has excelled him in the practical wisdom and discrimination of character with which he illustrates the case of those professors, weak in faith, who are saved, but *scarcely*, as if through fire; and that of those, strong in faith, who are saved *abundantly*. Binney is our great *business-like* preacher of the Faith, in consistency with moral common sense. My limits afford space for the extract of only the following passage from the great oration to which I specially refer my readers:—

" If the passages I have expounded do not mean what they *say* (which is all I have brought out of them), what *do* they mean? If they mean what they say, that meaning is a truth; as such it must be in harmony with all other truth, whether we can perceive that harmony or not; and with the like condition, simply as a separate piece of truth, it is practically binding on the conscience of the Church. I firmly believe in Justification by Faith,—in the pardon of the sinner on the ground, exclusively, of Christ's glorious redemptive act. A thing this, purely gratuitous; in itself incapable of degrees; admitting, therefore, of no modification in different individuals in consequence of difference among them, but conferred upon all alike, in virtue of their union by faith with Him, whose work is the Divine reason for the blessing being bestowed at all. There is no doubt about all this; but depend upon it, whether you can see it or not, there is a harmony between this justification by faith and a judgment by works; and— whether you have yet found it or not—there is a principle somewhere, on which that harmony can be demonstrated. In some way or other, there is "a prize" of our "high calling" as well as "a gift" of God "through Jesus Christ." There is "a crown" in relation to which some may *so* run as to "obtain"—and some so, that another shall "take" it. There is a being saved—and nothing more; saved because *on* the foundation; saved, as it were, with difficulty, like "a brand plucked from the burning," that is—"so as by fire:" and there is a being saved "abundantly;" saved—and something more; saved and distinguished,—distinguished, because *to* the foundation has been "added" that which the Master will delight to recognise and honour." (pp. 170, 171.)

I have transcribed exactly from the original, observing the author's punctuation, dashes, italics, and signs of quotation. —He is not the man who will resent it as presumption that a younger brother remonstrate with him : Why allow the dull, indolent objector even the shade of apology, that the harmony is not clear; when the testimony of the Augsburg Confession, adopted by all the churches of the Reformation, is, to reason and common sense, clear as sunshine, that the *person* of the *believer* being accepted *his works* are accepted too, and rewarded; or, as I have popularised it in my illustration, that having been *adopted* through faith, his works are rewardable as those of a son, and in proportion to his faithfulness ?

The Rev. Richard Watson's Sermons. I find not in the Institutes of this eminent Wesleyan divine anything to serve my present purpose. But he gives his testimony most satisfactorily in his sermon on Daniel xii. 13, The servant of God dismissed and rewarded (No. xxviii.) "That there are different rewards in heaven accords with our best ideas. Every man shall have his *own lot*. If the patriarchs and prophets, the martyrs and confessors, the apostles and evangelists, the experienced saints, those who have borne the burden and heat of the day, were to have no higher degrees of happiness than ordinary Christians, it would contradict our best notions of the divine government. But Jesus Christ himself has decided this question. Rule, thou who hast increased thy pounds to five, over five cities! and thou who hast increased thy pound to ten, rule thou over ten cities! And thus it is that every man, though he strictly deserves nothing, is in this distribution rewarded according to his work. Blessed is he who is faithful in little as in much! for God shall give him the true riches. This stamps an immense importance upon every moment of our time, and on every action of our life. We are either diminishing our *lot* or enriching it. Our actions are like seed sown in the earth, which must produce their harvest. "The harvest is the end of the world." "He that soweth to his flesh shall of the flesh reap corruption; but he that soweth to the Spirit shall of the Spirit reap life everlasting." (Works, vol. iii. p. 33.)

EPISCOPALIAN TESTIMONY.

Dr. O'Brien's (Bishop of Ossory's) Sermons, upon the Nature and the Effects of Faith.—(3rd edition, 1863).—The doctrine of Justification by Faith alone has never been pleaded more cogently in respect of rational and scriptural argument, and in respect of pious appeal more persuasively, than in this treatise, in defending it from the imputation that that doctrine relaxes the bonds of morality. Relaxes them! Why, the great Andrew Fuller, by appealing to facts, shows that the result is precisely the opposite—that it is the men who reject the doctrine that are the *loose*, and those who embrace it the *strict*, in their moral principles and observance of the divine law—explain the facts in whatever manner we may. Fuller explains them very satisfactorily (Socinianism and

Calvinism compared); but it is especially with Dr. O'Brien I am at present engaged.

He pleads especially the *derivative* argument as employed by the Erskines and Fisher; but he advances beyond them, and pleads the animating influence of the promise of Reward, in proportion to faithfulness, and *that* not merely a *quasi* reward of heavenly felicity being enjoyed, in necessary moral sequence, according to the qualification of the soul of the saint, in receptivity or susceptibility, through *culture in gracious habits* in this world,—but, a reward properly so called, directly and specially conferred by the Divine Father, in testimony of his approbation of *his child*, and delight in him, and as a recompence of his faithfulness—the Great Advocate standing by and displaying and pleading the excellence of *his brother*.
—But hear our learned and pious author (pp. 210, 211) :—

"Important differences in the condition of men hereafter would be the *natural result* of the differences of their moral state in leaving life: and this would be enough for my purpose. But we have good authority for referring some differences in their future lot to what we should call a more *direct appointment* of God. The notions of the eternal world, which are usually entertained, are well expressed by an eloquent writer, when he calls it 'an ocean of spirits without bottom and without shore.' But such vague notions of the world to come are not scriptural. The Bible, without supplying much food for curiosity, gives us much more definite information. We know from it that there exist now among the inhabitants of heaven wide distinctions. We are told of differences in angelic *natures*—as angel and arch-angel, seraphs and cherubs—which we must suppose real and important, though we can form no clear idea of them. But, besides these, we read of distinctions among them of *rank* and *authority*, of which we can form better conceptions—thrones, and dominions, and principalities, and powers (Col. i. 16; Ephes. i. 21; 1 Peter iii. 22).— And the glimpses which we are given of the state of *saints* hereafter hold out very clearly the existence and maintenance among them of the like distinctions. We have the Apostles sitting upon thrones with Christ, judging the twelve tribes of Israel (Matt. xix. 28, Luke xxii. 30). We have the place of highest dignity on his right hand, and on his left hand, in his kingdom reserved for those for whom it is prepared by the Father (Matt. xx. 23). And other instructions will, probably, of themselves come into your minds, tending to establish the same fact—that, though, in the spiritual world, they that are wise shall shine as the brightness of the firmament, and they that turn many to righteousness as the stars for ever and ever (Dan. xii. 3); yet it shall be there as in the natural world, where one star differeth from another star in glory (1 Cor. xv. 41)." See also Witsius and Dr. Sommerville.

There is a great deal more of similar admirable matter in Dr. O'Brien's illustrations. But he turns round and engages a long earnest lecture with admonishing his hearers (the theological students of Trinity College, Dublin), that, neither for themselves personally, nor as guides for others, they permit this promise of reward, as addressed to their self-love, to gain the ascendancy, as a motive to obedience, above a sense of gratitude—in such a manner as almost to neutralise his previous pleadings for the influence of the promise. This astonishes me. One of the great difficulties of my ministry has been to get out of men the *virtue* of having their *self-interest* excited by the promise of *God's reward*—his promise of salvation from misery and reinstatement in his family *for* faith—his promise of exaltation in glory *for* well-doing—the love of well-doing for its own sake, being acquired by the *habit* originally generated by a respect to *self-interest,* and throughout sustained by it. Disinterested virtue is a fancy; the doctrine of it is a *craze*—it is much worse—it is an invasion of the prerogative of the self-sufficient God, who holds all his creatures in such subjection to Himself, that to please Him and gain his favour be the grand motive of their conduct. Whence the ordination? Because their virtue pleases Him, and because it is best for themselves.

I close this *recension* of testimonies with mingled feelings; *first,* with a kind of shame and chagrin that I should have produced so little in favour of my present doctrine, in respect of modern testimonies (though not in respect of the more ancient and venerable); but, *secondly,* with a degree of self-complacence that I have produced so much as will strengthen brethren, who are oppressed by the fears of the opprobrium of a pretentious zealotry, to burst the bands of the ignominious bondage and preach the gospel without mutilation.

APPENDIX.

(B)

GETHSEMANE.

WHAT WAS THE CUP FROM THE DRINKING OF WHICH CHRIST PRAYED IF IT WERE POSSIBLE HE MIGHT BE SAVED?

In answer to this question, I have maintained in the text that it was not the cup of the impending sufferings of the Cross, but that of the Mental Agony which He presently endured, even while He prayed. There are a number of illustrations, however, which, for brevity's sake, it was necessary to exclude from the general discussion; but which, from their interest and importance, and from their having been sketched after considerable study, I judge it proper to preserve and introduce here.

There are only these three ways in which any one who conceives that Christ prayed for deliverance, if possible, from the threatening cross, can consistently explain his having done so: First, that he did not know that it was necessary He should suffer a violent death, or one so exceedingly violent, in order to complete the work of redemption to which He was commissioned; Second, that He did know it was necessary, in order to that end; but that He prayed for being absolved, if possible, from the commission; Third, that He knew that it was necessary, and was well-resolved, whatever might be required, to implement the commission;

but that momentarily his human nature gave way, in the near prospect of the horrors of the cross, so as to extort the expression of the wish that, if possible, He might be saved from them.

The last of these attempted explanations, as being the more common one, I have exposed in the text, as greatly derogatory from the character of our Lord; and here only add the censure of the eminent Markland, as quoted with approbation by Bloomfield in his Digest (Matt. xxvi. 38); only, I do not say that I concur in the last sentence, for I do not clearly understand it; nor in the distinction betwixt the cup and baptism, which I doubt: "This is generally interpreted of our Saviour's praying that He might *not die*. God forbid it should be so! when He knew and always declared that He came into the world on purpose *to die*. The mistake has been owing to interpreters not distinguishing between *cup*, which is in this place, and *baptism*. By this latter is meant death; by the former a smaller portion of distress, less than death. The distinction is made Matt. xx. 22, and elsewhere; and by all the evangelists in this place. Now, our Saviour hath Himself told us that God always heard Him; and we know from Heb. v. 7, and Luke xxii. 43, that He *was* delivered from this *present terror* that was upon Him, whatever it was: but we know that He was not delivered from *death*.—It is difficult to know what this *cup* was. We may be certain from the circumstances that there was something very terrible in it. But as it is not clearly revealed what it was it seems not necessary for us to know any further than it was not *death*, which we may be *sure of:* at least to one who is persuaded of the truth of this opinion, it would be blasphemy to say that our Saviour prayed to be delivered from death."

I know not that any one has had recourse to the Second explanation; and have given it a place only for exhausting logical possibilities. I therefore dismiss it.

There remains for consideration the First: that Christ did not know it was *necessary*, that, as the ordained Redeemer, He should undergo the violent death of the cross. This is the only consistent ground on which any one can explain that He prayed for deliverance from its *apparent* approach: and many who hold the third opinion, when they commence with protesting their belief that from being of a Divine nature He knew most certainly that it was necessary, yet proceed to say that being of a human nature He, in a state of tremor, prayed as if it were possibly escapable—I say not—far from it, for many of them are good men—that they are guilty of what Markland seems to impute to them; but this I say, that in this matter they do Christ's character not a little dishonour, and that as interpreters they shamefully stultify themselves.

But some one may ask might not the human soul of Christ, which notwithstanding the union with the Divine nature, was not omniscient, have been at the time ignorant of the necessity of his death; so that, whether in a state of tremor, or of full self-possession He might consistently pray for being saved from it, if it were possible? The question is most reasonable; and I answer it by saying that so far as the union of the two natures, or the Hypostatical Union, as theologians call it, is concerned, the human nature *might have been* ignorant; but that, *historically*, no proof of any thing is clearer than that it was *not ignorant*, but deeply and thoroughly convinced that such was the divine ordination in the mediatorial scheme and arrangements. It is chiefly the latter part of this answer in which we are at present interested; but in order to appreciate the evidence fully it is necessary to make some explanation of the former.

Among other heresies which troubled the Church in early times were these two, that of Apollinaris, who taught that in the Incarnation of our Lord the Divine nature was substituted in the place of an intelligent soul in the human nature —and that of Eutyches, who taught that the Human nature was *absorbed* by the Divine. Both opinions were denounced and condemned by councils convoked to judge on them; and the testimony has been kept up in modern times, as when the Westminster Divines say in their Confession that "two whole, perfect and distinct natures, the Godhead and the Manhood, were inseparably joined together in one person, without *conversion, composition,* or *confusion.*" And, again, in their Larger Catechism (the word *entire* only being left out in the Shorter), they say that "Christ, being the Eternal Son of God became Man, and so was and continues to be God and Man in two *entire, distinct* natures, and one person for ever." Notwithstanding all this, how frequently do we not hear in the popular preaching of the present day representations made, and expressions used which consist only, if not with the Apollinarian *substitution,* at least with the Eutychian *absorption!** according to which the identity of the human soul of Christ, both morally and intellectually, is virtually destroyed; so as to render nugatory the doctrine of his example as man, and greatly to impair the doctrine of his sacrificial sufferings; for on the hypothesis of his soul being *deified* by the absorption, He could suffer but slightly; even though the Eutychian heresy were not carried its legitimate

---

* I do not make this charge in ignorance of the Patristic distinction called *oikonomia.* *See* Hill's Lectures, B. iii., chap. viii.

length, that the body was absorbed too, so that all appearance of suffering was in appearance only.

But it is especially the manner in which the notion of absorption affects the views which men take of the *intelligence* of the soul of Christ, in which we are at present concerned. It leads them to regard it as having been omniscient. You may hear it preached and expounded any Sabbath that He knew perfectly well that the fig-tree (Mark xi. 13) was barren; but that He *affected* ignorance, or assumed the appearance of it, that He might have an opportunity of displaying his power! It might as well be said, as the genuine Eutychians did, that the *hunger* was affected too. But let us limit our considerations to the *intelligence*. All theologians among us, worthy of the name, agree that it is as impossible to communicate the divine property of omniscience to the soul, as that of omnipresence or ubiquity to the body. And that the intelligence of the soul of Christ was limited, we have express Scriptural testimony. The union of the two natures was as close and intimate at his birth as in his manhood; and yet it is said of Him, that "the child grew, and waxed strong in spirit;" and again, that He "increased in wisdom;" indicating a progress inconsistent with omniscience. (Luke ii. 40, 52.) He went to the fig-tree "*if haply* he might find anything thereon" (Mark xi. 13.) Of the day decreed for his returning in glory to this world, He declared He was ignorant (Mark xiii. 32); and, which is specially to my present purpose, He prayed for *something* in Gethsemane, of the possibility of granting which He was not sure.

Some will ask, of what avail, on these principles, was the divine to the human nature? I answer, that by the union it relatively and officially dignified it, though it did not communicate to it its divine properties. The divine nature was to the human what the golden crown is to the king. That crown does not communicate golden properties to the king's flesh and mind, but leaves them just the same as the flesh and mind of his subjects: it only officially aggrandizes him. In like manner the divine nature of Christ, as crowning the human, royalizes it, when yet it continues a human nature the same as that of "his brethren." The sufferings of Jesus of Nazareth were those of a Divine King, and of a Divine King is the authority of the Crucified Galilean.* Dr. Dick, recently professor of Theology to the United Presbyterian Church, and universally reputed as one of the soundest and most judicious of theologians, says—"The doctrine of the Church in all ages—and it is agreeable to Scripture—has been that the two natures of Christ, although hypostatically united, continue distinct; that each retains its peculiar attributes; that omnipotence, omniscience, and omnipresence, though predicated of the *person*, belong to Him only as God; and that the *sole effect of the union with respect to the human nature is to enhance the value of its actions*, which are truly the actions of the only Begotten of the Father. To suppose that divine properties are communicated to the human nature is to confound the Creator with the creature; and it may be confidently affirmed to be impossible even for Omnipotence to make that infinite which is finite." (Lecture xci.)

Whence then the intrinsic excellence of Christ's human nature? This is a question which preachers in general have not studied with accuracy, so that they are confused in mind themselves and leave the people perplexed. Let it be observed, then, that all that superior excellence was *of the endowment*

* Discourses by the author: First Series, No. 2. On the Incarnation and he Secret of believing it.

of the Father. This will not be disputed so far as *native* and *constitutional* excellence is concerned: and there are two reasons wherefore the endowment was made to the greatest extent of which human nature is capable. First, in "preparing a body" (Heb. x. 5), by which I understand an entire humanity, for his well beloved Son, we may be certain that He consulted for that Son's honour; so that He should not be so intimately associated with what was ignoble or common, and not of the very highest order. But, Secondly, He must have had respect to the worthiness of the Sacrifice; in the acceptance of which for the sins of mankind his government might be vindicated in its righteousness: and when from amid the universal degeneracy no lamb was to be found sufficient for this end, He all but *created* one; only employing a mother of the old race, that the identity of nature might be preserved. These requirements of the case being considered, we cannot wonder that Christ was *constitutionally*, through the Father's operation, all that magnanimous model of Humanity which his life and character display.—In these sentiments, respecting the native constitution of our Lord's human nature as being of the Father's origination, all will concur; and it is the confused or inaccurate views which prevail of the source of his qualifications for his office *after his birth* which I complain of and reprehend. And I maintain that these were as much of the Father's endowment as was the native constitution. The scheme of Redemption required this, inasmuch as He appeared as the Father's *Servant*, with his commission "sealed" by Him, and directed and upholden by Him in all the work. Accordingly, all the superior wisdom of Christ, his miraculous power, and his moral purity, are throughout the Scriptures of both Old and New Testaments uniformly ascribed to the endowment of the Father by the Holy Ghost, qualifying Him for his work; just in the same *manner*, though in *measure* unequalled,* in which He qualified Moses

* John iii. 34. "God giveth not the Spirit by measure, to Him;" not making his human soul omniscient, as all the older theologians explain; but qualifying Him *profusely* for the mediatorial office.

Turretin, Loc. xiii. Q. 13, proposes the question, Was the soul of Christ from its creation, so replenished with knowledge that there was nothing of which it was ignorant, or which it could learn? He answers in the negative; arguing both from the nature of the case, and express declarations of Scripture, Luke ii. 52, Mark xiii. 32, Heb. ii. 17; iv. 15—and answering objections founded on John xxi. 17, Matt. xii. 25, Col. ii. 3.—The Popish Doctors distinguished the knowledge possessed and acquired by Christ's human nature as being of three kinds, Beatific, Infused, and Acquired. By the Beatific they signified such intuitions as the glorified saints will enjoy; (Matt. v. 8,)—by the Infused, such as was communicated by the Holy Ghost—and by the Acquired, such as He gained by common ratiocination and experience. Turretin dismisses the first as incongruous with Christ's state of humiliation, in which He was *viator* and not *comprehensor*—on the way, and not having yet *attained*. To Acquisition he ascribes not a little —to Infusion, a relative *plenitude*—relative to his Mediatory character and office, but not absolute—only what was needful to endow Him profusely for his present work.—Some may wonder why Turretin, Pictet, and others showed such earnestness in illustrating and contending for the *limitation* of the state of the intelligence of the humanity of Christ. It is easily explained: they did so, First, in vindication of their own characters, as rational and pious men, who did not ascribe divine properties to a creature nature :—Secondly, because in their controversy with Arians and Socinians they could not defend the doctrine of Christ's Divinity, from objections made to it on the ground of a number of Scriptural testimonies and representations, which plainly indicate the *limitation*, except on the principle of their referring them to His *creature* nature. (That man who is thoughtful, and has any logic in his head, must sink down into Unitarianism or worse, who does not observe the distinction, that, in the Incarnation of the Son of God, the human nature was not endowed with divine properties, but only officially and royally magnified by the union) :—Thirdly, because in a humanity, endowed with divine attributes, they could not find a suffering sacrificial victim, as an atonement for sin: not to speak of other attributes, even the clear shining of omniscience would have so influenced Jesus of Nazareth as to render Him almost insensible to pain. He could not have been what He was, a Man of Sorrows :—Fourthly, the contention against the corporal presence in the Mass of Popery and the Eucharist of Lutheranism, in both cases implying an ubiquity or omni-

and all the other prophets, and in which He endows with grace all his saints. It is enough that I quote the two following passages as a specimen of a great multitude. Isaiah xlii. 1, " Behold my Servant whom I uphold: mine Elect, in whom my soul delighteth ; I have put my Spirit upon Him : He shall bring forth judgment unto the Gentiles." Heb. ix. 14, " How much more shall the blood of Christ, who through the eternal Spirit offered Himself without spot to God, purge your conscience from dead works ?"

Mark, therefore, where we now stand in respect of the main subject of illustration. Since Christ's human nature was not made omniscient by its union with the divine; and received its knowledge by gift after gift of his Father's Spirit, it *might have been*, so far as the constitution of his person is concerned, that that night in Gethsemane He did not know that his death was absolutely necessary—that it was something the knowledge of which the Spirit, howsoever lavish in its communications, had for wise ends withholden from Him, and that, therefore, He might consistently pray that He might be saved from the threatening evil. That *might have been* the case, howsoever strange the withholdment of the knowledge might have appeared to us.—But *was* it the case ? The matter is not one of speculation as to probability or improbability. It is a question of facts. Is there *historical* evidence that at the time He presented that prayer He was indubitably certain that He must suffer a violent death, and that it was impossible for his Father to exempt Him from the drinking of that bitter cup ?—I answer as before, that if Scriptural

presence of Christ's humanity, contributed to the zeal of Calvinistic Theologians in opposing all superstitious notions which corrupted the doctrine of our Lord's distinct though co-related manhood.

evidence can prove anything it proves this; and that to represent Him as, notwithstanding, praying for exemption, if possible, is an imputation to Him of that which I leave Markland to characterise.

When I proceed to adduce the Scriptural evidence of the manner in which the mind of Christ was impressed with the conviction that a violent death was decreed for Him, some may be ready to say that the exercise is superfluous, there being none who doubt the fact; but from the particular point of view at which I institute the inquiry, I trust they will feel interested by the freshness of the illustration, and not only be settled in the belief of the truth for which I at present specially contend; but be strengthened in the faith of the great atonement, when they see that our Lord's death was *essential* to the fulfilment of his Mission as a Saviour.

The investigation is directed especially to the state of Christ's convictions after He entered on his public ministry at the 30th year of his age, during the time which preceded his death; as it is only of the state of his mind during that time that we have any certain information, with the exceptions of the general intimation that as a child "He waxed strong in spirit, filled with wisdom," and that "the grace of God was upon him;" and of the record of a particular incident when He was twelve years old. (Luke ii. 40-52.) But there is not a little which we may *infer*, with considerable probability, respecting his life before He was manifested to Israel. Take into consideration these two natural elements of the case, at work— First, That Christ's human nature, as we have seen, was constitutionally of the best type of humanity. There is a tradition, and it is not an improbable one, that even his personal bodily appearance was remakable for its dignity and grace, accounting in some measure for his popularity; and some interpreters have thought that there is a reference to this in the words of that special Messianic Psalm, "Thou art fairer than the children of men" (xlv. 2.) But whatever there may be in this, it cannot be questioned that his native intellectual capacity was of the highest order. Consider, Secondly, the character of the Mother. How lamentably has not the idolatry of Rome prevailed with Protestants to reduce the Virgin Mary to the position of being merely a decent, pious, respectable person! On the contrary, I maintain that she was the most excellent type of womanhood to be found in all Israel, which is tantamount to saying, in all the world. "She was blessed among women," not so much in the sense of being so *fortunate* as to be selected for the highest honour, as of being worthy of the preference. We may be certain that it was no merely respectable person whom God selected to be the Mother of that member of the human family with whom He united so closely his only Begotten Son—no one merely respectable with whom his Spirit had such intimate communion in effecting the Great Incarnation. That the Virgin was morally eminent there can be no doubt; but that she must needs have been eminent for her intelligence also will appear as we proceed with the illustration.

Here then are the two parties—the child and his mother: reflect how matters would proceed naturally; and that they did proceed in the common order of education, though *quickened* more than usual by the ordinary influences of the Spirit, there is every reason to suppose. The child, like other children, needed a mother's teaching, and God had provided one well-qualified for the task. There was much of which it is said, "she kept all these things, and pondered them in her heart" (Luke ii. 19 and 51); and there were many of them for the communication of which her son, howsoever precocious, was not qualified, in the earlier stage of childhood; and for a few years she must have limited her instructions to general lessons of piety, and narratives of Hebrew worthies, and very specially of the great King David, who was a forefather of his: and then she would tell him that God had promised He would send another King like David, but much greater, from among David's children, to be called Messiah, to set all things right in Israel, and to make the whole world holy and happy: she would proceed and tell him that many good and wise people expected that God would send this wonderful King soon, the world having grown so bad and having so much need of Him; and who knows, she would say, but that He may be born already, and living in secret somewhere, to come forth soon from some lowly cottage, like David from the sheepfolds?—This is no fancy picture: it *must have been* in some such way that Mary proceeded with her great charge in training the childhood of the world's Redeemer. And how interested her apt scholar must have been, especially in her representations of the promised Deliverer—saying, tell me now, mother, something about King Messiah! It was his future Self whom she portrayed; and although He knew not, his mind was acquiring principles which contributed much to enable Him to turn the ideal of his mother into an active reality in his own conduct.

The time comes when she must reveal the secret.— When would it be? Making all allowance for the native superiority of his mind, and the forwardness of his education, it could not be much sooner, I think, than the eighth year of his age that He was capable of having the communication made to Him. She prayerfully ponders the matter, and resolves. She says she has something wonderful and of particular interest to Himself to tell Him, and retires with Him to the innermost chamber of their dwelling. What a season of emotion it must have been for both? She tells him that He himself is that Son of David— the Messiah, with thoughts of whom He has been so much engaged. She gives Him the evidence at first in a general way, to be detailed afterwards. She tells Him of the appearance of the angel to her, and his salutation, and that his birth was miraculous; so that Joseph is not his father, but that He is a Son of God. She tells Him of the angel's appearance to Joseph, of her visit to Elizabeth, of the shepherds at Bethlehem, of the wise men from the East, of Simeon and Anna, and the warning dreams of Joseph.— This, or parts of it, might be sufficient for the time.

What must have been the amazement, and all the other tumultuous feelings excited in the youthful mind of Jesus by these revelations of his mother it would be vain to conjecture. It is enough for our present purpose to conclude that by about the eighth year of his age, it was the settled conviction of his mind that He was the predicted Messiah. At what time the conviction was produced, growing into such consciousness as that which is in many instances evinced, particularly in the gospel of John, of his human nature being allied in personality to the divine, does not appear; but that at that early age He was thoroughly convinced of his Messiahship, there can be no reasonable doubt; and, thenceforward, the study of the character, work, and fortunes of that Messiah, so far as they could be ascertained from the prophecies, must have been for Him one of the deepest personal interest. With what earnestness and diligence, He and his mother and good Joseph, who was fully in the secret, must have pored over and pondered these prophecies—waited for any references in the services of the synagogue—and inquired at their more intelligent neighbours what were their views and expectations of Messiah! When we discover Him at twelve years of age at Jerusalem, in the Temple, "sitting in the midst of the Doctors, both hearing them and asking questions," how stupid it is, not to say profane, to represent Him, as is sometimes done, as humbling their pride and perplexing them by a display of his ingenuity? Instead of that, He was with much concern engaged, now that He had an opportunity of converse with learned men such as He could not find at Nazareth, in learning from their views of the promised Messiah, what should be his own work and reception when the time of his manifestation to Israel arrived. Accordingly, when remonstrated with by his mother for lingering behind among those men, He replied, "Wist ye not that I must be about my Father's business?" What business? Evidently the work of Messiah which was before Him. I notice, by the way, that this calling God his Father evinces his clear conviction of the truth of his mother's account of his divine Paternity. The rest of the company "understood not the saying." But Mary understood it well; and laid it up among others in her heart. (Luke ii. 41—51.)

It being established then that from early years Christ's mind must have been interestingly occupied with the studies of the prophecies concerning the Messiah as containing some account of what was decreed for Himself,—coming round to that point with which we are at present more particularly engaged, I appeal, if it was possible for Him to pursue that study without becoming deeply impressed by the conviction that, though great was the glory to which He would ultimately be advanced, it was a path of sorrow, tribulation, and violent death by which He would be conducted to it. It is sufficient to refer, as instances, to the prediction of Isaiah, that he should be "brought as a lamb to the slaughter" (liii. 7), and to that of Daniel, that "Messiah shall be cut off" (ix. 26). To the two disciples to whom He revealed Himself on their way to Emmaus, He said, "O fools, and slow of heart to believe all that the prophets have spoken: Ought not Christ to have suffered those things, and to enter into his glory?" (Luke xxiv. 25, 26.) How unjust this rebuke would have been, if He himself had not thus interpreted the prophecies, in those days when his circumstances were even more favourable for study than theirs?

There was large time for his mind being thoroughly imbued with the conviction, that, on being manifested to Israel, He should be subjected for a season to a life of great affliction, terminating in a violent death. But He must be a mature man; both that his sacrifice might be that of a sufficient representative of humankind, and that He might be qualified from experience to be our sympathising High Priest. So for a number of years He works as a mechanic for his daily bread, many reflections intermingling with his work. At hours of respite from labour, He converses with his mother and pious neighbours ; visits the poor and helps them, so far as his means enable him,—we may be sure of that; attends the synagogue, in the way of fulfilling all righteousness, but takes no active part in its ministrations, as in the honest interpretation of the Scripture, He might make premature revelations of Himself, as appears from what is recorded Luke iv. 16-22. He never *amuses* himself, except with little children; we may also be sure he did that.

Finally, He is constantly pondering the prophecies of the Messiah, meditates much, and prays much, both at home, and up among the rocks of Nazareth.

Having attained to the full vigour of manhood—*being matured*, He waits expectantly for the *signal:* and lo ! the echo of the voice of one crying in the Wilderness, " Prepare ye the way of the Lord, make His paths straight." He hastens away from Nazareth to meet the Baptist; and having been baptised, as He prayed, " Lo ! the heavens were opened to Him," and John " saw the Spirit of God descending like a dove and lighting upon Him, and remaining on Him : and lo ! a voice from heaven saying, This is my beloved Son, in whom I am well pleased."—Thus was he inaugurated and anointed Messiah. But besides being by this effusion of the Spirit fully qualified for the work before Him, it is probable that then, if not for the first time, there was communicated to his soul that conviction of which I have already spoken, amounting to a species of consciousness of the fact, of His human nature being allied in personal union with the divine nature of God's Eternal Son.

Not just yet, however, is He to be manifested to Israel. He must make proof of his qualifications for the office with which He has been invested. So He is led up into the wilderness to hold personal conflict with the Enemy, whose works He is commissioned to destroy. (1 John iii. 8.) He returns victorious: and mark now in what aspect, as his special characteristic, He is in the First Act of Manifestation set forth for the contemplation and faith of Israel, yea, of the whole world : it is the key note of the Gospel.

John i. 29. " John seeth Jesus coming unto him ; and saith (unto his disciples), Behold the Lamb of God, which taketh away the sin of the world !"

I dispute not at present with those who say that the significance of the emblem lies in His taking away sin by *wisdom* of doctrine, and *holiness* of example, qualities which these experts in natural history say are characteristic of such lambs as they are acquaint with! My appeal is to those who believe that the Heaven-inspired designation, whether the Baptist himself understood it or not, proclaimed Him a *sacrificial* victim for the expiation of sin by the suffering of death : and my appeal is this, If it be possible to conceive of Him as praying in Gethsemane, to be delivered, if possible, from that lamb-like *condition* on which, from the very first, a claim is made for Him on the world's dependence, love, and obedience?—Probably Christ himself heard the proclamation of his divinely-appointed Herald : at all events it must have been soon reported to Him, or communicated by inspiration : And even to Him who had heretofore meditated so much on the necessity of Messiah's death—how impressive, if I may not say startling, the proclamation must have been? Returning somewhat exultant from his victory in the wilderness, when He might reasonably calculate on his being hailed with felicitations, and some word about "the glory that should follow," He is contrariewise met with the proclamation of his doom, as a Lamb appointed to slaughter. Deeply must this sentence of death have descended into his soul. It is no longer for Him merely a deduction from the prophecies. The living voice of the Heaven-commissioned Harbinger has pronounced it.

Charged with his high commission, and burdened in heart with his death-doom, He returns to Nazareth ; but makes there in the first instance only a partial manifestation of his character and office, at the marriage supper in Cana— reserving the first public assertion of his claims for the occa-

R

sion of the Feast of the Passover, the national celebration of which, at Jerusalem, was approaching;—an occasion most fitting for making the assertion: and how strikingly, yet appropriately, He made it! It is difficult to determine which of the Messiah's offices of Prophet, Priest, and King was most signally displayed, when on entering Jerusalem He immediately proceeded to the Temple and cleared his Father's House of those who had made it a house of merchandise. (John ii. 11.)—But I refer to this at present, chiefly because it is introductory to what follows, and which is pertinent to the subject more immediately under illustration. Being asked for a sign of the authority by which He then acted, He answered and said unto them:

John ii. 19, " Destroy this Temple, and in three days I will raise it up."

The answer itself, and the other circumstances in which it is made are remarkable; but that to which I direct attention at present is the *time* of it. On this, *the very first occasion*, properly, of his being publicly manifested, He indicates how fully possessed his mind was with the conviction that, as the Messiah, He must undergo a violent death. Neither the Jews in general, nor the disciples, understood at the time that "He spake of the temple of his body:" but He himself uttered the words with the clearest conception of its being decreed for Him that those Jews should put Him to death. I reiterate, that He thus expressed Himself at the first opening of his mouth in public. The subject was one *essential* to his Messiahship.

Nearly contemporaneously with this declaration made publicly in the temple, there was one made in private which indicates still more particularly the state of his convictions. It was on the occasion of this Passover, at the opening of his ministry, that He was visited privately by Nicodemus for explanations and instruction. "He did not commit Himself," specially to the promiscuous multitude. But here was an honest inquirer, intelligent and cultivated beyond any one perhaps with whom Christ met confidentially, in the whole course of his ministry. It is accordingly remarkable to what an extent He unfolds to him the system of salvation. He gives him an epitome of the Gospel—The necessity of Regeneration by the Spirit—Salvation by Faith in the death of Himself, the Son of God, sent to this world as the gift of His Father—and the necessity of a life of holiness and good works as consequent on this Faith. It is the second of these points in which we are at present especially interested. Through the portal, then, of Regeneration having introduced Nicodemus into his church, what is the first object He presents to his view?

John iii. 14, 15. "As Moses lifted up the serpent in the wilderness, so must the Son of Man be *lifted up*, that whosoever believeth in Him should not perish, but have eternal life."

By the expression of being "lifted up," we have express Scriptural authority for understanding that He not only signified a violent death, but the special form of the death, as being that of Crucifixion. (John xii. 32.) Whether he had learned this from Psalm xxii. 16, "They pierced my hands and my feet," or by a direct communication of the Spirit, we cannot determine; but it is enough for our present purpose to be assured that at this entrance on his public ministry, before there were any appearances of opposition to his claims (for the asking of Him what was his authority, at the temple, was a reasonable demand) He nevertheless was not only convinced but openly and privately declared his conviction, that He would be put to death, as an event essential to his Mission and not merely accidental, or one for which another could be substituted. He *must be lifted up.*

Shortly after this first passover of his Manifestation He returned to Galilee, in which region (excepting short occasional excursions into other parts of Judea, and presenting Himself at feasts in Jerusalem), he expended his earthly ministry; till about five or six months before the last passover, He left Galilee on his way to "accomplish his decease." There is a difference of opinion among Harmonists, as they are called, of the four Gospels, in calculating the length of time which his Ministry occupied; some contending that it was protracted for three years and a half, from his baptism, so as to include four passovers; others, that it was accomplished in two years and a half, so as to include only three passovers. There is also a want of agreement in their arrangements of the chronological order of his sayings and doings.

Let it be observed that my present argument is but slightly dependent for its force on our determining whether his ministry was of the longer or shorter duration. My principal object is to show that in either case He was *throughout* deeply impressed with the conviction that *He must be lifted up* on the cross, so that it was impossible for Him to pray in Gethsemane, that He might be delivered from it if possible; and that his mind was so pervaded by it that it broke forth at times in utterances which we might have called *inopportune*, in respect of the *present* fitness of his auditories to understand them and receive them; but the remembrance of which was most important for them, and the record of which is most important for us. As for the chronological order of the utterances—first, all are agreed that those which I have already noticed were given at the first passover; and, secondly, that those which I have enumerated at the conclusion were given in the course of the six months before the last, whether third or fourth. The others which I have classified as *intermediate* were given earlier or later in his ministry, in the order I think in which I have enumerated them.

Intermediate Utterances—
Mark ii. 19, 20, And Jesus said unto them, Can the children of the bridechamber fast, while the Bridegroom is with them? But the days will come, when the Bridegroom shall be taken away from them, and then shall they fast in those days. (Compare John iii. 29.)

Matt. x. 38, He that taketh not his cross, and followeth after me is not worthy of me. (Both Campbell and Bloomfield maintain that there is a reference here to his own literal cross, though the term may be extended figuratively to all the sufferings of his disciples.)

John vi. 53, Except ye eat the flesh of the Son of Man, and drink his blood, ye have no life in you. (Signifying a reliance by faith on his sacrificial death.)

John vii. 6, Then Jesus said unto them, My time is not yet come. (That the time referred to is that of his death is made plain by the Evangelist's note at verse 30th—Then they sought to take Him: but no man laid hands on Him, because his hour was not yet come.)

John viii. 28, Then said Jesus unto them, When ye have lifted up the Son of Man, then shall ye know that I am He.

John ix. 4, I must work the works of Him that sent me, while it is day; the night cometh, when no man can work. (Compare John xi. 9.)

Matt. xii. 40, As Jonas was three days and three nights in the whale's belly, so shall the Son of Man be three days and three nights in the heart of the earth. (Compare Matt. xvi. 4; Luke xi. 29.)

Luke xiii. 32, 33, Go ye and tell that fox (Herod), Behold, I cast out devils, and I do cures to-day and to-morrow, and the third day I shall be perfected, . . . for it cannot be that a prophet perish out of Jerusalem. (That his being *perfected* consisted in his having accomplished his work by death, when his hour had come, will scarcely be questioned). (Compare John vii. 6; xi. 9.)

John x. 11, 15, The good shepherd giveth his life for the sheep, . . . and I lay down my life for the sheep.

Utterances during the last Six Months—
Matt. xvi. 21, From that time forth began Jesus to shew unto his disciples, how that He *must* go unto Jerusalem, and suffer many things of the elders and chief priests and scribes, and be killed, and be raised again the third day. (And when Peter presumed to dissuade Him, He rebuked him with indignation, as speaking in opposition to the counsel and decree of God.) (Compare chap. xvii. 22; xx. 18; Luke xviii. 31; Mark viii 31.)

Luke ix. 30, 31, And, behold, there talked with him two men, which were Moses and Elias: who appeared in glory, and spake of his decease which He should accomplish at Jerusalem. Matt. xvii. 9, And as they came down from the mountain, Jesus charged them, saying, Tell the vision to no man, until the Son of Man be risen again from the dead.

Matt. xvii. 12, Elias is come already, and they have done unto him whatsoever they listed: likewise shall also the Son of Man suffer of them.

Matt. xx. 28, The Son of Man came not to be ministered unto, but to minister, and to give his life a ransom for many.

(This was uttered at the conclusion of the scene when, on his way to Jerusalem, the mother of Zebedee's children, supposing He was about to erect his kingdom, besought Him to show them a preference.)

John xi. 9, 10, Are there not twelve hours in the day? If any man walk in the day, he stumbleth not, because he seeth the light of this world. But if a man walk in the night, he stumbleth. (His day was fast declining, but an hour of it yet remained; and disregarding the remonstrance of the disciples, he hastened up to Bethany to awake Lazarus, knowing that his enemies, though lying in wait for him, would not just yet prevail. But He immediately retired, and did not return till the close of his day.

Sun setting came. Having arrived at Bethany, there were yet six days before that fatal Passover. He employs them with the utmost diligence; every morning going to Jerusalem to address the assembled multitude at the temple. That multitude was of such a promiscuous character that He could not opportunely discourse much of his approaching death; and yet He publicly gave one utterance in relation to it, which, perhaps more than any other which He ever gave, provoked his enemies: He, in a manner challenged them to do their worst; as it was now his time to go to his Father.

Luke xx. 13-19. Then said the Lord of the vineyard, What shall I do? I will send my Beloved Son: It may be they will reverence Him when they see Him. But when the husbandmen saw him, they reasoned among themselves, saying, This is the Heir: come, let us kill Him. So they cast Him out of the vineyard, and killed Him. . . And the chief Priests and the Scribes the same hour sought to lay hands on Him; for they perceived He had spoken this parable against them. (So they plotted with Judas. He knew of it all: and could easily, at the last hour—even on leaving the guest chamber, instead of going to Gethsemane, have made his way across the Jordan and eluded them. Yea, even when surrounded by the armed band sent to apprehend Him, He says his prayer to his Father would have brought legions of angels to his aid—" But how then," He says, " shall the Scriptures be fulfilled, that thus it must be"—" the cup which my Father hath given me, shall I not drink it?") (Matt. xxvi. 54; John xviii. 11.)

John xii. 23, 24, 27. Jesus answered them, saying, The hour is come that the Son of Man should be glorified. Verily, verily, I say unto you, Except a corn of wheat fall into the ground and die, it abideth alone: but if it die, it bringeth forth much fruit. . . . Now is my soul troubled; and what shall I say? [Shall I say] Father, save me from this hour? [Nay] For this cause came I unto this hour. Father, glorify thy name! (Observe, this solemn protest is given exactly and pointedly against what some represent Him as having done shortly afterward in Gethsemane.)

Matt. xxvi. 10, 12. Why trouble ye the woman? for she hath wrought a good work upon me; for in that she hath poured this ointment on my body, she did it for my burial. (This utterance was given at a feast to which He had been invited in Bethany, after retiring from the day's labour in Jerusalem—possibly the day of his triumphant entrance. But so certain is He of the nearness of "his hour" that He must cast a gloom over the festivity, by assuring them of his burial being close at hand.)

Utterances in the Guest Chamber—
John xiii. 1. Now before the feast of the Passover, when Jesus knew that his hour was come that He should depart

out of this world unto the Father, having loved his own which were in the world, He loved them unto the end. (Compare Matt. xxvi. 17; Mark xiv. 17; Luke xxii. 14.)

To quote the whole of the utterances in that Guest Chamber which indicated the manner in which his mind was impressed with the conviction that his death was imminent, would require a transcription, almost bodily, of the whole of the evangelical narratives. As has been stated in the text, the entire scene resembles that of one who, on a death-bed, for the last time, addresses his children or friends. As before I notice especially his Institution of the ordinance of the Supper, to be observed in all future ages as commemorative of his death.

At the conclusion, therefore, of this recension of evidences of the manner in which our Lord's mind was affected by the conviction, pervading his whole life, that He must die a violent death, I appeal with augmented force, If it be possible to conceive of Him, on any moral principle, praying at last, even momentarily, for an escape from that death, even submissively with the condition, if it were possible, when all along theretofore He had been convinced it was impossible? —Although, however, my principal object in making the recension was the strengthening of the above appeal, I have had a subordinate one. I trust the concentrating of the evidence into one view, of Christ having felt that his dying as a ransom for sin was the grand object of his Mission, will promote the belief of the characteristic doctrine of Christianity—that of his expiatory sacrifice.

www.ingramcontent.com/pod-product-compliance
Lightning Source LLC
Chambersburg PA
CBHW021350230426
43666CB00006B/466